I0434912

THE TRANSFORMATIONAL LEADER
PRESIDENT
GOODLUCK E. JONATHAN

Dr. LeVonder P. Brinkley

© 2015 by Dr. LeVonder Pheon Brinkley
1st Printing

All rights reserved including the right of reproduction in whole or in part in any form or by any means without the prior written permission of the author, except by a reviewer who may quote brief passages in a review to be printed in a newspaper, journal or magazine.

The Library of Congress Cataloguing-In-Publication Data:

Title ID: 5246849

ISBN-13: 978-1506170169

BISAC: Political Science / Public Affairs & Administration

Printed by CreateSpace, an Amazon Company

Manufactured In

USA   Great Britain   Europe

Reprints may by Ordered at   https://www.createspace.com/5246849

OTHER PUBLICATIONS BY

DR. LEVONDER PHEON BRINKLEY

Co-author of the #1 Best Selling Book Series-
Wake Up…Live the Life You Love "Seizing
Your Success" (Dr. Deepak Chopra,
Dr. Wayne Dyer and Others)

A Path Called Purpose…
Can Only Be Traveled by Passion

Burn with Passion to Journey on Purpose

The Gratitude and Action Journal
(Volumes I, II, III, IV)

Real Estate Investment 101-
"How to Get the Contract"

Mental Disability across the Life Span –
(Thrive Counseling & Coaching Journal of Boston
Psychotherapists and Life Coaches) - June 2008

The Vibrational Frequency of Love and Above-
(Dissertation)

LeVonder Pheon Brinkley

The H. E. Goodluck Ebele Jonathan

"A Transformational Leader...

identifies the needed change, creates a vision to guide the change through inspiration, and executes the change with the commitment of the members of the group."

Transformational leadership is defined as a leadership approach that causes change in individuals and social systems. In its ideal form, it creates valuable and positive change in the followers with the end goal of developing followers into leaders. Enacted in its authentic form, transformational leadership enhances the motivation, morale and performance of followers through a variety of mechanisms. These include connecting the follower's sense of identity and self to the mission and the collective identity of the organization; being a role model for followers that inspires them; challenging followers to take greater ownership for their work, and understanding the strengths and weaknesses of followers, so the leader can align followers with tasks that optimize their performance....

Table of Contents

Foreword

A lot has been written and said about the effectiveness of the Jonathan administration since they took office in 2009. Many people's negative views of this administration have found abundant examples of things that continue to go wrong as evidence and they point to decayed infrastructures, rampant corruption, lack of adequate energy supply, and insecurity among others. What detractors and critics of this administration minimize or fail to give fuller considerations are that these issues are very intractable for any one administration to tackle, and secondly, these issues existed long before this administration came to power. What this administration has failed to do, in my view is blow their own horns; loudly tout their achievements, large and small, but this does not align with the personality of our current truly civilian President, unaffiliated to the military since President Shagari.

People have criticized President Jonathan for not being like previous blustery, obnoxious and ruthless military henchmen. They think he is not addressing instability and insecurity in the country because he has not sent soldiers to troubled regions to "wipe everyone out". Nigerians are accustomed to military leaders who wipe out people and whole communities, rather than engage in constructive dialogues. Indeed democratic societies do engage its enemies, no matter how detestable we think they or their actions may be. I do not want a President disposed to draconian, undemocratic measures to solve problems within its borders. Previous leaders who wiped out whole communities merely postponed the issues, only to have them re-emerge in different forms, perhaps from different regions.

This President has walked a very tight rope and has the fortune of leadership in an age of free press and social media explosion where minute events are magnified and plastered across global stages. He has been caricatured on every platform, yet he has not censured, rebuked or sought retributions, unlike other leaders. His administration recalibrated the economy to ensure that Nigeria's place in the global economic stage is recognized, which now attracts increased investments. President Jonathan has been accused of being slow to address the Boko Haram issue. As President he is responsible for everything that happens in the country, but Presidents rely on security experts and law enforcement personnel tasked with ensuring the country's safety and security. Detractors cry that he has not visited Chibok to meet families of kidnapped girls. I contend that going to Chibok would have not freed a single girl; in fact going to Chibok will only be theatrical and might embolden the kidnappers, affirming that the President's presence imbues certain cache and legitimacy to their diabolic aim to de-stabilize the country. International allies with vanguard technologies and satellites are yet to unearth the whereabouts of the kidnapped girls. President Goodluck Jonathan has repeatedly affirmed his commitment to find and free the Chibok girls, but his detractors fail to hear or believe him.

Finally, President Jonathan has the constitutional rights to run again in 2015, just like anyone else who is eligible and affiliated with a legitimate political party in Nigeria. Our role as citizens is to vote for candidates of our choice.

In this work Dr. Brinkley speaks of her Vision for Nigeria as a fully developed nation and highlights some of President Jonathan's many accomplishments that are moving our nation towards a stabilized developed country, with absolute security and peace among all Nigerians regardless of Tribal or religious affiliation.

Dr. Chamberlain Diala,
Health Policy Analyst

Dr. Chamberlain Diala is a Health Development Specialist. He lives and works in Washington, DC.

Prologue- I Envision a Nation

I write this book as an Appointed Ambassador for Peace of the Universal Peace Federation. President Jonathan has aligned himself with our organization and for this reason I write this book to share all I have learned about this Transformational Leader.

Nigeria has arrived at a critical junction in its own history. On the one hand, the election of President Goodluck Jonathan represented a movement for reform and a major step up to a higher standard of governance. But on the other hand, there are old-school corrupt former politicians and retired military leaders who want to return to power to sabotage the president's agenda. There are radical elements of both Islamists and Christians who are ready to launch their own holy wars against the government and each other which could cripple the country's hope for rapid change and development. Recalling that His Excellency, President Goodluck Jonathan in his October 1, 2013 address to the nation announced the setting up of a committee to develop a framework for a national dialogue to address the several challenges facing the nation, and the follow up inauguration of the committee as well as call for submission of memorandum by the Committee. The Universal Peace Federation, an international NGO with a Special Consultative Status at the United Nations ECOSOC, convened a special meeting of the Ambassadors for Peace in Abuja and Lagos to deliberate on the terms of reference provided by The Presidential Advisory Committee on National Dialogue.

The Ambassadors for Peace commends His Excellency President Goodluck Jonathan for the response to the agitations of the Nigerian people for an opportunity for an all-inclusive dialogue of citizens across the nation and noted with keen interest the fact that the President has moved the focus of the nation through the proposed dialogue from fighting one another to bringing all of us together to dialogue with the hope that we can identify our differences and commonalities in order to forge genuine national reconciliation.

The Ambassadors for Peace recommended that the year 2014 be proclaimed at all dialogue sessions as a Year for National Unification of Nigeria. Each dialogue session should endorse the need for a Ministry for Interreligious Affairs, Ministry for Family Affairs and also consider the replacement of State of Origin with Place of Residence and that all Nigerians should be regarded as citizens of the country and not indigenes of tribes. In seeking to formulate a new national philosophy for the nation, the Ambassadors for Peace recommended the consideration of the core universal ethic of Living for the Sake of Others to be the nation's guiding philosophy. UPF also attached the UPF's 5 universal principles for peace and dialogue, which we consider as relevant for consideration and endorsement by the Committee as the guiding principle at all sessions of the nationwide dialogue.

- We are one human family created by God. The way to rise above the pursuit of self-interest is to recognize our common humanity, given to us by our Creator. Just as a parent can intercede in the disputes of children, the parental heart originating from the Creator can help us resolve the differences that exist between and within our nation, cultures and religions.

- The highest qualities of the human being are spiritual and moral in nature. Human beings long for truth, beauty and goodness. Life's deepest meaning and purpose can be found through that pursuit. Each person has an eternal spirit that transcends physical life. Spiritual principles are to be practiced in this life so that we are prepared for the eternal world.

- The family is the "school of love and peace." In the family, the most basic personal and public virtues are learned. Understanding the family as the school of love helps us to recognize that family is the most essential institution. The foundation for a healthy family is a faithful, committed marriage.

- Living for the sake of others is the way to reconcile the divided human family. By practicing living for the sake of others, we become other-centered rather than self-centered. The essence of good character is true love expressed through unselfish actions.

- Peace comes through cooperation beyond the boundaries of ethnicity, religion and nationality. Lasting peace cannot be achieved through political compromise alone but requires addressing the root causes of conflict. Transcending racial, religious and ethnic barriers is an imperative of our time. Faith can give people the power to forgive, and the love to overcome even generations of hatred, resentment and violence.

On behalf of the Ambassadors for Peace of the Universal Peace Federation, who met in special sessions to deliberate on the terms of reference provided by the Presidential Advisory Committee on National Dialogue and made the above recommendation, we wish to convey our appreciation and pray that the Committee's work should gain the support of all Nigerians and should be able to move the nation forward in our desire to become a global leader in the 21st century and beyond.

While thanking the President and Commander In Chief of the Federal Republic of Nigeria and the Presidential Advisory Committee on National Dialogue for this unique opportunity to contribute to the building of a new Nigeria, please accept the assurances of our highest regards and considerations. As an Ambassador of Peace and the alliance of the Transformational Leader Goodluck E. Jonathan with UPF, I have a vision for the Great Nation of Nigeria, the strongest economy in Africa!

NIGERIA

I SEE A NATION... Nigeria as independent, hopeful, and free as on that fateful day on October 1, 1960 when independence was gained from the United Kingdom ...where children play **PEACEFULLY** in their yards; their parents live, worship, and work in peaceful co-existence with their brethren without regard for their tribal or religious differences.

I SEE A NATION... that has **DEVELOPED** and **STABILIZED** its government in all areas. Its citizens are healthy; its economy is strong- it has a middle class to stabilize the economy; government funding is at a minimum of 26% as recommended by the United Nations Educational, Scientific and Cultural Organization for a developed country; its products and manufactured goods are superior and it imports less, but exports more; it produces more than enough food to meet the needs of its citizens; an absence of gender discrimination in the work place; high environmental standards; high health standards, hospitals are well funded, doctors and medical personnel are skilled; youth are involved with dialogue in the government, youth empowerment programs are in place to ensure youth employment; inter-religious dialogue in the government; highway systems are more than adequate; persons who misappropriate funding receive punitive consequences; strong anti-crime programs; strong anti-drug programs; waste recycling and management programs; adequate and sustainable energy power; large corporations move there to bring in better employment; patriotism of the wealthy exists to help the country and less fortunate countrymen. People no longer love money and power more than they love their country and its citizens.

I SEE A NATION...that has overcome **SECURITY CHALLENGES.** The challenges are no more than those in America and the UK. There is internal national security, food security, financial security, and personal security. The Anti-terrorism law is implemented and perpetrators of heinous crimes are punished, which has created an absence of Terrorist groups and gangs.

Government leaders and the citizens cooperate with President Jonathan on his Transformation agenda – they have ushered in a new era of PEACE, HOPE, and FREEDOM for all Nigerians. This book will highlight MANY of the changes that have been made by his administration to accomplish his Transformation Agenda to ensure the transformation to PEACE, STABILIZATION OF DEVELOPMENT, and NATIONAL SECURITY.

Dr. LeVonder Pheon Brinkley, Inspirational Author and Appointed Ambassador of Peace of the Universal Peace Federation (upf.org).

Our Transformational Leader:

H.E. President Goodluck E. Jonathan

(Photo from http://house2houseng.com/category/slider/)

H.E. President Goodluck Ebele Jonathan, in a statement on the post-election crises in some parts of the country said:

> As president, it is my solemn duty to defend the constitution of this country. That includes the obligation to protect the lives and properties of every Nigerian wherever they choose to live. I will defend the right of all citizens to freely express their democratic choice anywhere in this country; to enjoy every freedom and opportunity that this country offers without let or hindrance. I assure all Nigerians that I will do so with all powers at my disposal as "president, commander-in-chief." I have ordered the deployment of security personnel to troubled parts of the country. I have directed the reinforcement of security in all parts of the country. I have authorized our security services to use all

lawful means including justifiable force to bring immediate end to all acts of violence against fellow citizens.

On May 5, 2010, Vice-President Goodluck Jonathan was sworn in as President of the Federal Republic of Nigeria. On the 6th of May 2010, he became Nigeria's 14th Head of State. He cited anti-corruption, power and electoral reforms as focuses of his administration. In 2011, President Jonathan launched the Transformation Agenda. The Transformation Agenda is based on a summary of how the Federal Government hopes to deliver projects, programs, and key priority policies, from 2011 to 2015 coordinated by the National Planning Commission.

Among several others, the core objectives of President Jonathan's Transformation Agenda is underlined by the desire of the present administration to promote social and economic changes through the optimization of economic growth; develop a knowledge-based economy and enhance security of lives and property; accelerate growth, provide employment and reduce youth restiveness as accentuated by the spiraling wave of violence and criminality all over the country. (*http://www.vanguardngr.com/2011/08/jonathan%e2%80%99 s-transformation-agenda-the-perspective-of-ibb- others/#sthash.S8AG3MC1.dpuf*)

SUSTAINABLE GROWTH AND DEVELOPMENT FOR A STABILIZED NATION

SUSTAINABLE GROWTH AND DEVELOPMENT OF NIGERIA

President Jonathan's transformation Agenda is moving with record pace!

The Transformation Agenda

- **Increase the GDP**

- **Decrease Inflation**

- **Crude Oil Tankers**

- **Foreign Investors**

- **Solar Power Plants**

- **Renovate Rail lines**

- **Agriculture Reform**

- **E-wallet for Farmers**

- **Affordable Mortgages**

- **Emergency Gas Supply**

- **Bulk Electricity Trader**

- **Completion of Major Ports**

- **Increase per Capita Income**

- **Gas Pipelines to Power Plants**

- **Reservoir and Portable Water**

- **Initiatives for Longevity of Life**

- **Renovation of Federal Airports**

- **Quality and Access to Education**

- **Domestic Crude Oil Production**

- **Increase Insurance Policy Holders**

- **More Affordable and Quality Housing**

- **National Counter-Terrorism Strategy**

- **Venture Capital for ICT**

- **Entrepreneurship**

- **Increase in Mobile Phones and Internet**

- **Access Major Roads, Expressways, & Bridge Projects**

- **Transform Nigeria, the largest producer of cassava in the world, into the largest processors of cassava in the world.**

Before & After

President Jonathan's Administration

(Pictures from Oronto Douglas Special Adviser to the President on Research, Documentation and Strategy and the Website at transformationagenda.com/before-after/)

Before & After

President Goodluck Jonathan and the transformation of Nigeria

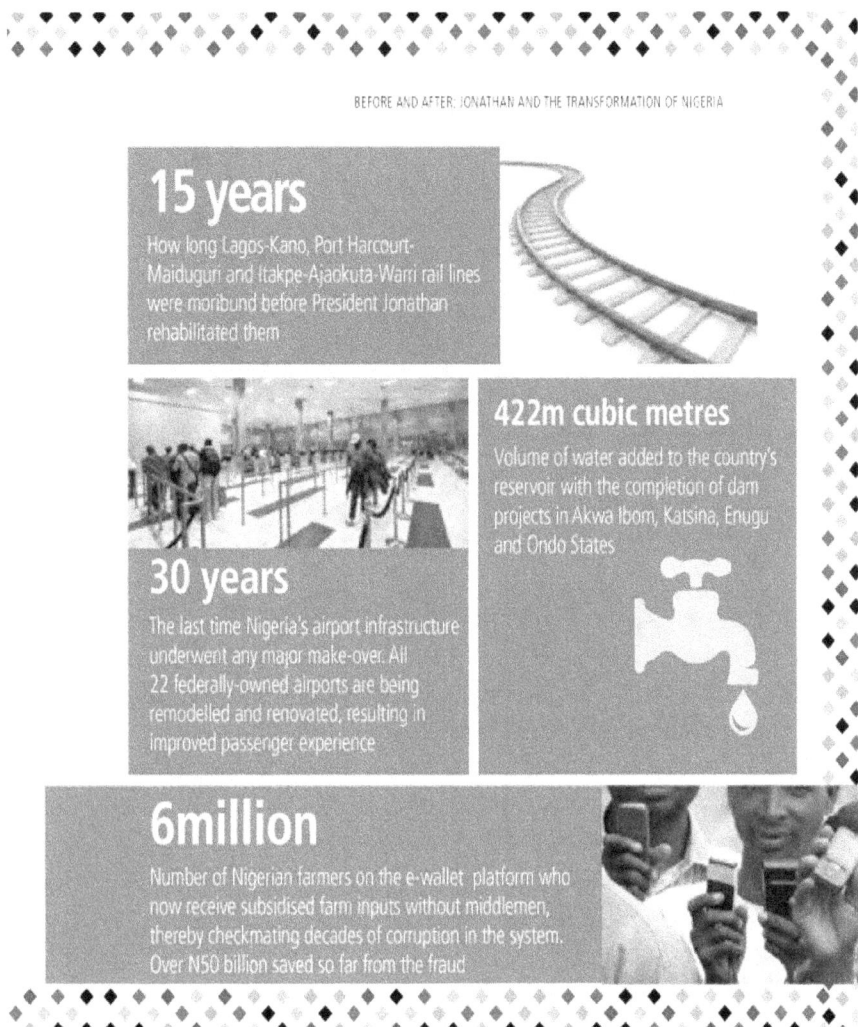

BEFORE AND AFTER: JONATHAN AND THE TRANSFORMATION OF NIGERIA

15 years
How long Lagos-Kano, Port Harcourt-Maiduguri and Itakpe-Ajaokuta-Warri rail lines were moribund before President Jonathan rehabilitated them

422m cubic metres
Volume of water added to the country's reservoir with the completion of dam projects in Akwa Ibom, Katsina, Enugu and Ondo States

30 years
The last time Nigeria's airport infrastructure underwent any major make-over. All 22 federally-owned airports are being remodelled and renovated, resulting in improved passenger experience

6million
Number of Nigerian farmers on the e-wallet platform who now receive subsidised farm inputs without middlemen, thereby checkmating decades of corruption in the system. Over N50 billion saved so far from the fraud

- **Railways renovated for the first time in 15 years. Pre-Jonathan Era- Less than 1 million people traveled by rail. Jonathan Era- With the rehabilitation of the rail lines system, nearly 6 million people travel by rail.**
- **30 years since airports have been repaired or renovation.**
- **422m cubic meters of water added to reservoirs by completion of dams.**
- **6 Million farmers accessing E-wallet eliminating corruption.**

130,000 barrels

Volume of crude oil production per day by the Nigerian Petroleum Development Corporation (NPDC), compared to nothing before

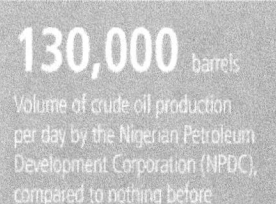

400%

increase in Silo capacity under President Jonathan

7 Days

How long it takes to clear trouble-free cargo, down from 39 days before. Number of agencies at the ports has been reduced from 13 to 7, streamlining bureaucratic and financial requirements for clearance and decongestion

CARGO

5million

Passengers carried by rail, compared to 1 million some years ago

- Pre- Jonathan Era: 0 Barrels of Crude production per day.   Jonathan Era- 130,000 Barrels per day.
- 400% in Silo Storage Capacity
- Cargo cleared in 7 days compared to 39 days before, reducing cost.
- Pre-Jonathan Era: 1 million Passengers traveled by Rail.
- Jonathan Era: Nearly 5 million Passengers travel by Rail.

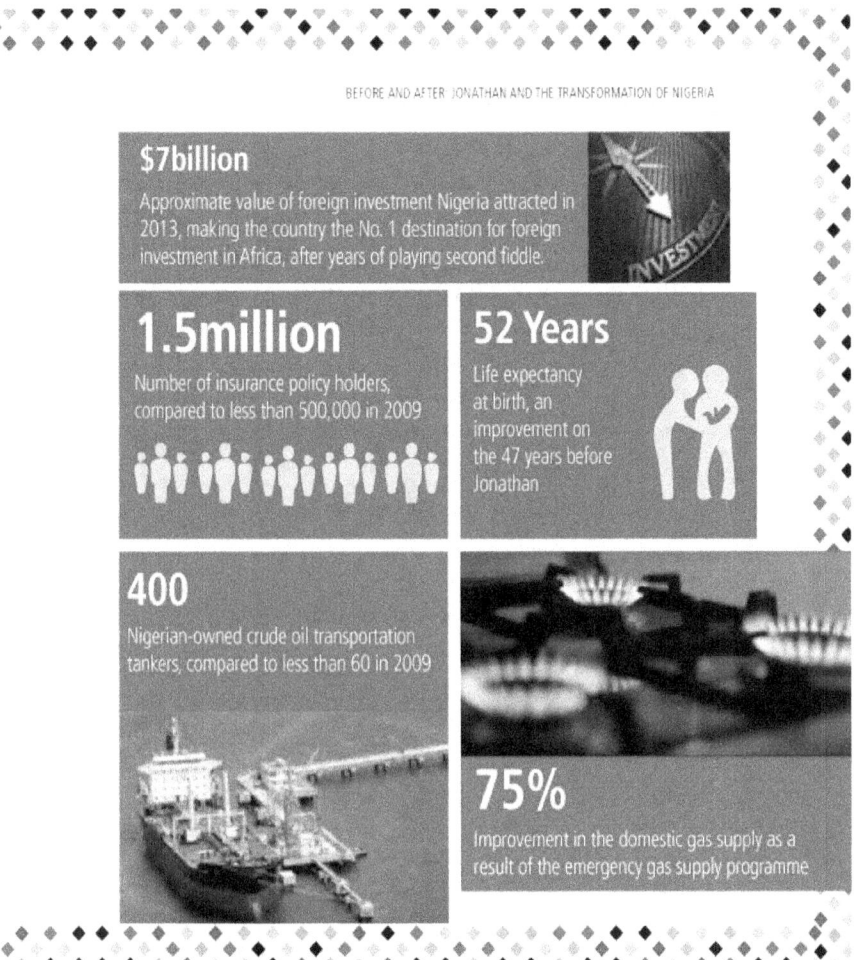

BEFORE AND AFTER JONATHAN AND THE TRANSFORMATION OF NIGERIA

$7billion
Approximate value of foreign investment Nigeria attracted in 2013, making the country the No. 1 destination for foreign investment in Africa, after years of playing second fiddle.

1.5million
Number of insurance policy holders, compared to less than 500,000 in 2009

52 Years
Life expectancy at birth, an improvement on the 47 years before Jonathan

400
Nigerian-owned crude oil transportation tankers, compared to less than 60 in 2009

75%
Improvement in the domestic gas supply as a result of the emergency gas supply programme

- **$7 Billion in Foreign Investment attracted to the Country.**
- **Pre-Jonathan Era: < 500,000 Insurance Policy Holders Jonathan Era: 1.5 Million of Insurance Policy Holders**
- **Pre-Jonathan Era: Life expectancy at Birth was 47. Jonathan Era: Life expectancy at Birth is 52.**
- **Pre-Jonathan Era: < 60 Nigerian owned Crude oil tankers.   Jonathan Era: 400 Nigerian owned Crude oil tankers.**
- **75% Improvement in the Domestic gas supply as a result of the emergency gas supply program.**

ECONOMIC TRANSFORMATION

- **Pre-Jonathan Era: GDP was 169bn
  Jonathan Era: GDP is 283**
- **Pre-Jonathan Era: Per capita income was $1091 (IMF)
  Jonathan Era: Per capita income is $1721 (IMF)**
- **Pre-Jonathan Era: Inflation rate was 15%
  Jonathan Era: Inflation rate is 8% due to increase in
  local food production.**

BEFORE AND AFTER: JONATHAN AND THE TRANSFORMATION OF NIGERIA

ECONOMIC MANAGEMENT

INDICES	PRE-JONATHAN ERA	JONATHAN ERA
GDP	$169bn (2009)	$283bn (2013)
Per capita income	$1091	$1721 (IMF)
Non-oil Exports	N1.5tr	N1.45tr (2013 Q1-Q2 only)
Non-oil Revenue	N848bn	N1.34tr
Non-oil GDP	N17tr	N20tr (2013 Q1-Q3 only)
Tax revenue	N2.19tr	N4.8tr
Inflation rate	15%	8%

helped mainly by the increase in food production locally

Agricultural Policy Reforms:

At the core of the agricultural transformation agenda are some major policy and institutional reforms to help sanitize the sector, eliminate corruption and re-position the sector to better performance, and restore credibility for the sector before Nigerians and the international community.

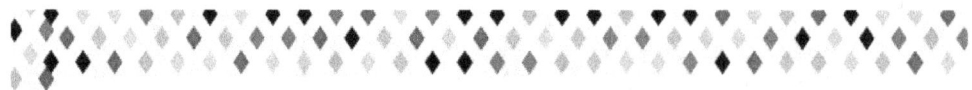

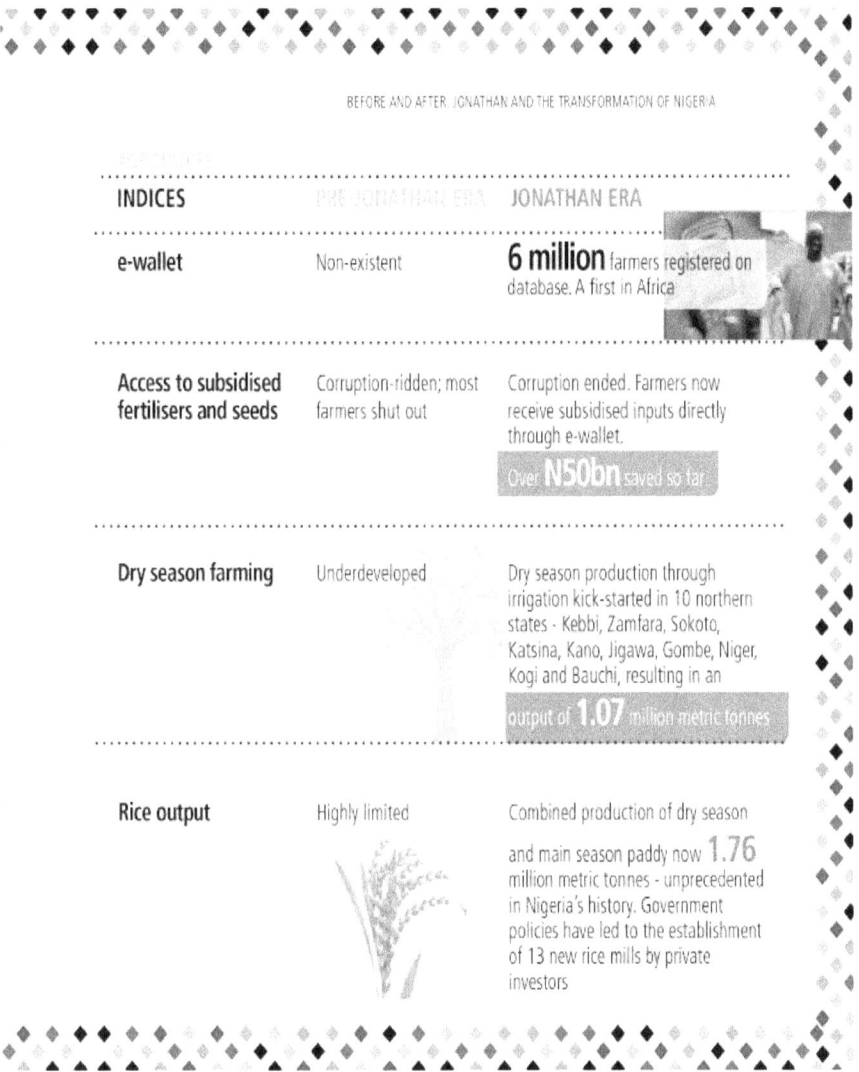

BEFORE AND AFTER: JONATHAN AND THE TRANSFORMATION OF NIGERIA

INDICES	PRE-JONATHAN ERA	JONATHAN ERA
e-wallet	Non-existent	**6 million** farmers registered on database. A first in Africa
Access to subsidised fertilisers and seeds	Corruption-ridden; most farmers shut out	Corruption ended. Farmers now receive subsidised inputs directly through e-wallet. Over **N50bn** saved so far
Dry season farming	Underdeveloped	Dry season production through irrigation kick-started in 10 northern states - Kebbi, Zamfara, Sokoto, Katsina, Kano, Jigawa, Gombe, Niger, Kogi and Bauchi, resulting in an output of **1.07** million metric tonnes
Rice output	Highly limited	Combined production of dry season and main season paddy now 1.76 million metric tonnes - unprecedented in Nigeria's history. Government policies have led to the establishment of 13 new rice mills by private investors

The goal of Rice Transformation agenda is to achieve self-sufficiency in rice production and complete substitution of imported rice by year 2015.

Achievements
• Successfully secured a US investor (Dominion farms) to invest $40 million to develop a 30,000 ha rice farm in Taraba State, hich will be the largest rice farm in Africa. Rice mill for the farm has been ordered, 50 young Nigerians have been trained

in Kenya for 5 months on commercial rice production, and the planting of the farm started in December 2012.

• New fiscal measures announced by Mr. President raising tariff for brown rice, and levy on imported finished rice, to encourage local rice production.
• In response to the new fiscal measures for rice and the rice transformation action plan, 13 new private sector mills were established in the last 12 months, buying and processing local paddy. The total capacity of the new mills is 240,000 MT.

• High quality local rice rolled out on commercial scale by Ebony Rice, Ashi Rice, Mikap rice and Umza Rice. The local rice made a strong entry into the market, displacing imported rice due to high quality, taste and price.

BEFORE AND AFTER: JONATHAN AND THE TRANSFORMATION OF NIGERIA

INDICES	PRE-JONATHAN ERA	JONATHAN ERA
Production of high quality cassava flour to substitute imported wheat in the baking industry	Fledgling	Expanded
Agricultural orientation	Largely subsistence	Launched a self-employment initiative under the Youth Employment in Agriculture Programme (YEAP) called the "nagropreneur" programme. This scheme, designed to encourage youth to go into commercial agriculture as entrepreneurs, plans to develop over 750,000 young nagropreneurs by 2015
Wheat	High import	Rapidly falling import

Cassava Transformation:

The goal of the cassava transformation programme is to turn Nigeria, the largest producer of cassava in the world, into the largest processors of cassava in the world. Government is aggressively expanding markets for cassava, through the development of high quality cassava flour to substitute for up to starch, high fructose cassava syrup and ethanol, 40% of wheat imports, dried cassava chips, native and modified.

President Jonathan launching the
40% High Quality Cassava Flour Bread
on November 30, 2011.

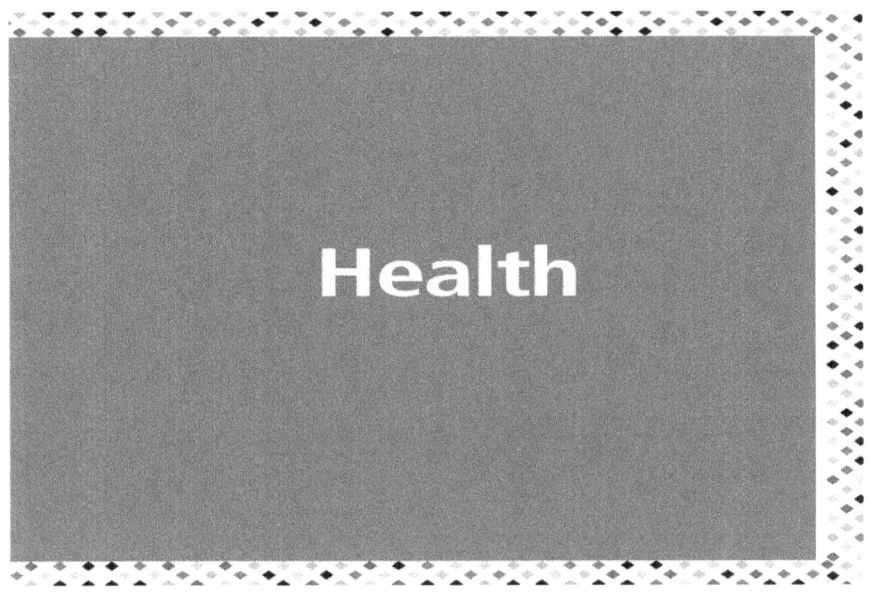

Over 433,650 lives were saved under the "Saving One Million Lives" Initiative by scaling up interventions: Maternal and Child Health; Nutrition; Prevention of mother to child transmission of HIV; Provision of essential commodities; malaria control; routine immunization; and the eradication of Polio.

- Established a Center of Disease Control.

- Reduced Maternal Mortality by 50%.

- Strengthened the capacity for Kidney Transplants.

HEALTH

INDICES	PRE-JONATHAN ERA	JONATHAN ERA
Life-Saving initiative	Nil	Under the "Saving One Million Lives" initiative, over 433,650 lives were saved from November 2012 to June 2013 through scaling up of six cost-effective interventions including Maternal & child health, nutrition, prevention of Mother to child Transmission (PMTCT) of HIV, Provision of Essential commodities, Malaria control, routine immunisation and eradication of polio
Nigeria Centre for Disease Control (NDCD)	Nil	Established
Maternal mortality	High	Dropped by 50% in four years
Malaria in children	Relatively high	Reduced
Capacity for kidney transplant	Fledgling	Strengthened with Lagos University transplant Teaching Hospital and University of Ilorin Teaching Hospital joining the league

LeVonder Pheon Brinkley

HEALTH

INDICES	PRE-JONATHAN ERA	JONATHAN ERA
Community-based health insurance scheme	Nil	**Established** in a number of communities in **12 states**, thereby granting medical access to poor Nigerians
Health insurance coverage	Less than 6%	Over **8%**
The National Immunisation Coverage	Less than 40%	Over **80%**
Under-5 mortality	157/1000 live births	down to **94/1000** live births
Maternal Mortality ratio	545/100,000	Down to **350/100,000**
Guinea worm disease	Affecting over 800,000 yearly	Eradicated
Curriculum for the training of paramedics	Nil	Established
Type-3 wild polio virus	Constant transmission	For the first time in the history of the country, there has not been any transmission of the virus for more than one year

1.07 metric tones

Increase in farm output following the introduction of dry season farming through irrigation in 10 northern states - Kebbi, Zamfara, Sokoto, Katsina, Kano, Jigawa, Gombe, Niger, Kogi and Bauchi in 2013

$1.2billion

Forex demand saved through local sufficiency in cement production

433,650

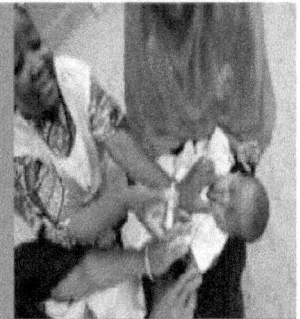

Number of lives saved under the "Saving One Million Lives" initiative from November 2012 to June 2013 through scaling up of six cost-effective interventions including Maternal & child health, nutrition, prevention of Mother to child Transmission (PMTCT) of HIV, Provision of Essential commodities, Malaria control, routine immunisation and eradication of polio

AVIATION

BEFORE AND AFTER: JONATHAN AND THE TRANSFORMATION OF NIGERIA

AVIATION

INDICES	PRE-JONATHAN ERA	JONATHAN ERA
New terminals for international airports	Nil	**Five** modern international passenger terminals Lagos, Abuja, Port Harcourt, Kano and Enugu
Safety and Navigational aids	Inadequate, obsolete	**Modernised** upgraded expanded nationwide
Accident Investigation and analysis laboratory	Nil	**Installation** of one in Nigeria. It is only one of the four in Africa and the only one in the West African sub-region
US Category 1 Certification	Nil	Attained

LeVonder Pheon Brinkley

INDICES	PRE-JONATHAN ERA	JONATHAN ERA
National Aviation Master Plan and Road Map	Nil	Developed, being implemented

Air safety	Partially implemented	Installation of cutting-edge navigational aids and Instruments Landing Systems (ILS), including runway lights and Total Radar Coverage (TRACON), to enhance air safety

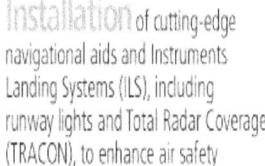

Airport infrastructure	Poor, obsolete	For the first time in over three decades, all 22 federally-owned airports are being remodelled, and renovated resulting in improved passenger experience

Cargo airport	Nil***	16 airports close to the nation's food baskets have been designated for perishable cargo to enhance preservation, conditioning and transportation of perishable cargo in accordance with international standards and best practice

RAILWAY SYSTEMS

- **BEFORE < 1 MILLION PASSENGERS**

- **JONATHAN ERA ALMOST 5 MILLION**

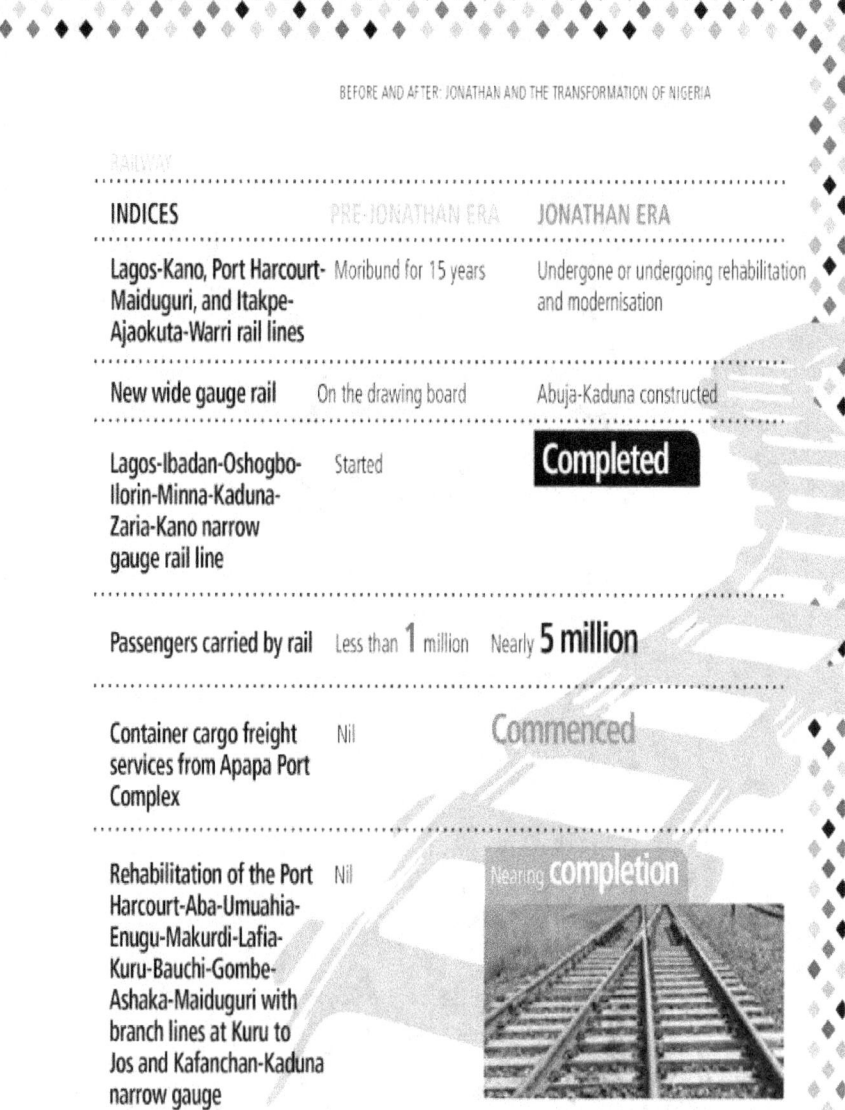

BEFORE AND AFTER: JONATHAN AND THE TRANSFORMATION OF NIGERIA

RAILWAY

INDICES	PRE-JONATHAN ERA	JONATHAN ERA
Lagos-Kano, Port Harcourt-Maiduguri, and Itakpe-Ajaokuta-Warri rail lines	Moribund for 15 years	Undergone or undergoing rehabilitation and modernisation
New wide gauge rail	On the drawing board	Abuja-Kaduna constructed
Lagos-Ibadan-Oshogbo-Ilorin-Minna-Kaduna-Zaria-Kano narrow gauge rail line	Started	Completed
Passengers carried by rail	Less than 1 million	Nearly 5 million
Container cargo freight services from Apapa Port Complex	Nil	Commenced
Rehabilitation of the Port Harcourt-Aba-Umuahia-Enugu-Makurdi-Lafia-Kuru-Bauchi-Gombe-Ashaka-Maiduguri with branch lines at Kuru to Jos and Kafanchan-Kaduna narrow gauge	Nil	Nearing completion

- **Pre-Jonathan Era: < 50% of population had access to portable water. < 250,000 passengers traveled by waterway.**

- **Jonathan Era: Nearly 70% have access to portable water. Over 1 million passengers travel by waterway.**

- **The completion of Dam Projects has added 422 metric cubic meters of water to the reservoir.**

- **Irrigation has more than doubled.**

- **Major Ports are completed or almost completed.**

PORTS

INDICES	PRE-JONATHAN ERA	JONATHAN ERA
Daily Port Operations	8 hours	Now **24 hours** for the first time since 1970 
Clearing time for trouble-free cargo	39 days	**7** days
Number of agencies at the ports	13	Now **7**, streamlining bureaucratic and financial requirements for clearance and decongestion

LeVonder Pheon Brinkley

WATER RESOURCES

INDICES	PRE-JONATHAN ERA	JONATHAN ERA
Access to potable water	Less than half of the population	Nearly 70% of the population. Seven water supply projects have been completed, providing additional 4.3 million Nigerians access to potable water
Irrigation projects	Mostly in the pipeline	Significant progress has been made on major projects such as the South Chad, the Bakolori Irrigation Project and the Galma dam
Dam projects	Mostly in the pipeline	Nine dams have been completed in Akwa Ibom, Katsina, Enugu and Ondo states to increase volume of nation's water reservoir by 422 mcm
Irrigated area	Less than 90,000 hectares	Over 200,000 hectares, leading to increased production of over 400,000 metric tonnes of irrigated food products
Farmers' access to irrigated land	Less than 200,000	Over 400,000 farmers

41

INLAND WATERWAYS

INDICES	PRE-JONATHAN ERA	JONATHAN ERA
Dredging of Lower River Niger from Baro (Niger State) to Warri (Delta State)	Nil	**Done,** allowing all-year navigation
Onitsha Port	Conceived	**Completed**
Baro Port, Lokoja Port and Oguta Port	Nil	**Nearing** completion
Number of passengers travelling by water per year	Less than 250,000	Over **1 million**

Pre-Jonathan Era: Production of 2 Million metric tons of Cement.

Jonathan Era: Production of 28.2 Million metric tons of Cement.

Developed a Master Plan for 100% local Sugar production.

President Jonathan has launched a National Industrial Revolution Plan on rice milling, sugar processing, cassava, manufacturing of consumer goods, cement, textiles, and petrochemicals.

Manufacturing

INDICES	PRE-JONATHAN ERA	JONATHAN ERA
Industrial revolution	Hazy	President Jonathan has launched the National Industrial Revolution Plan (NIRP) on the entire value chain of sub-sectors such agro-processing (e.g. rice milling, sugar procession, cassava for wheat flour and other products, etc., consumer goods manufacturing, cement, textiles, and petrochemicals)
Sugar policy	Hazy	Government has developed the Sugar Master Plan (NSMS) to provide roadmap for 100% local production of sugar
Cement production	Net importer	Net exporter. Nigeria has moved from producing 2 million metric tonnes of cement in 2002 to a capacity of 28.5 million metric tonnes. Saved over N200bn in the process
ECOWAS Tariff	Unfavourable	Nigeria has negotiated a strong Common External Tariff (CET) agreement with our ECOWAS partners which would enable us to protect our strategic industries where necessary

Armed Forces and Security have developed a National Counter Terrorism Strategy.

An Army Language Institute is in place to help Army personnel become bi-lingual in 2 years

A Dog training center has been established.

Army Armored Carriers have been built by the Army.

Warships have been built by the Navy.

Drones have been built by the Air Force.

ARMED FORCES & SECURITY

INDICES	PRE-JONATHAN ERA	JONATHAN ERA
National Counter Terrorism Strategy (NACTEST)	Nil	**Developed**
The Nigerian Army Language Institute	Non-existent	Institute established to make army personnel bi-lingual within **two** years
Dog Centre	Nil	**Established**
Local Armoured Personnel Carrier (APC)	Nil	**Built** by the Nigerian Army
Made-in-Nigeria warship	Nil	**Built** by the Nigerian Navy
Made-in-Nigeria drone	Nil	**Built** by the Nigeria Air Force

Pre-Jonathan Era: Inadequate Roadway systems.

Jonathan Era: Multi- Lane Highways and Expressways

ROADS

FLOODED OSHODI-APAPA ROAD

Before repairs...

After repairs...

INDICES	PRE JONATHAN ERA	JONATHAN ERA
Onitsha-Owerri and Vom-Manchok roads	On drawing board	**Completed**
Onitsha-Enugu and Lokoja-Benin roads	On drawing board	Under reconstruction and **expansion**
Lagos-Ibadan Expressway	On drawing board	**Reconstruction** and expansion works commenced
Second Niger Bridge project	On drawing board	Concessioned to Julius Berger/AIM consortium. Early works **commenced**
Mokwa-Bide Road, Akure-Ilesha Road, Sokoto-Tambuwal-Jega Road, Enugu-Abakaliki Road, Ogoja-Ikom Road and Vandekiya-Obudu roads	On drawing board	**Under** construction

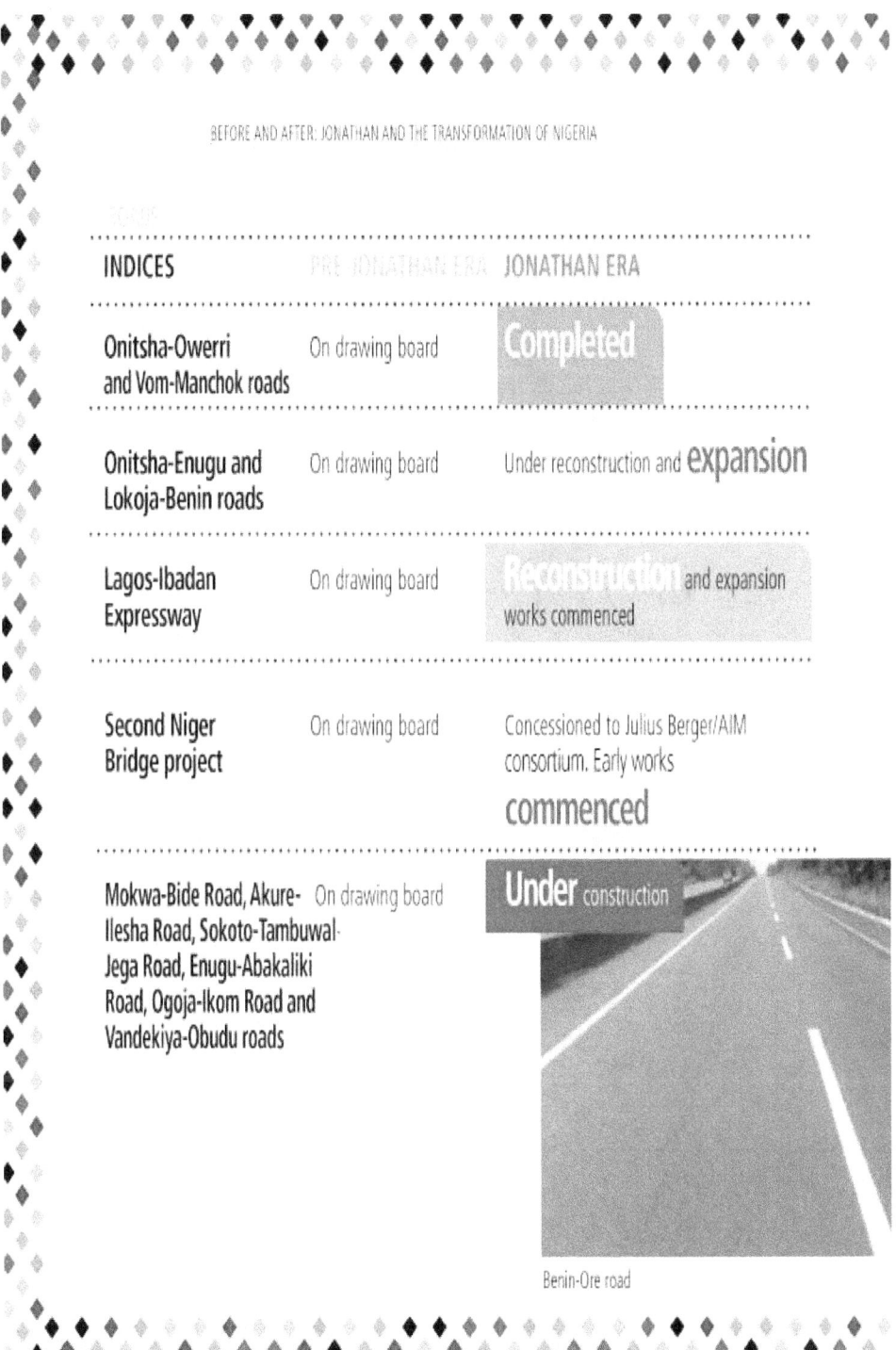

Benin-Ore road

ROADS

INDICES	PRE-JONATHAN ERA	JONATHAN ERA
Apapa-Oshodi Expressway, Benin-Ore-Shagamu Highway and Enugu-Port Harcourt dual carriage	On drawing board	**Reconstructed** or nearing completion
Kano-Maiduguri and Abuja-Abaji-Lokoja	On drawing board	Undergoing **dualisation**
Oweto Bridge across River Benue	On drawing board	**Constructed**

Kano-Maiduguri road Eastern Bypass

Pre-Jonathan Era: Passing % in Math and English 25.99

Jonathan Era: Passing % is 70.

125 Almajiri Schools now exist in 13 States and 275 more are being constructed.

Special Girl Schools are under construction in 27 States.

36 new universities will absorb students previously denied university admission and 58 Colleges of Education built.

101 Presidential Scholarships will be awarded for Innovation and Development.

100 Innovation Enterprise Institutions and 7,000 lecturers are being trained for post graduate studies to improve the quality of education.

Budgetary allocation for EDUCATION has doubled.

Fed. Gov. rehabilitated 352 Labs, constructed 72 new libraries.

Collaboration of Emmanuel University, Raleigh, NC USA with Amarachi Academy of Global Languages and Technology.

EDUCATION

INDICES	PRE-JONATHAN ERA	JONATHAN ERA
Almajiri schools	Nil	**125** schools built in 13 states; 275 more to go
Special girl schools	Nil	Under construction in **27** states
Federal universities	27	36, with 12 new universities (9 in the North, 3 in the south) established to enhance access to a Federal university across the country and absorb thousands of students who are denied university admission every year
Presidential Special Scholarships For Innovation And Development (PRESSID)	Nil	A total of **101** have been awarded to beneficiaries for training in top 25 universities in the world
Basic school enrolment	Less than 20 million	Over **30 million**
O'Level credit pass in English and Maths	25.99%	70%

EDUCATION

INDICES	PRE-JONATHAN ERA	JONATHAN ERA
Innovation Enterprise Institutions	Nil	Over 100 Innovation Enterprise Institutions have been licensed to provide alternative access to higher education through technical and vocational education and training
National Certificate of Education (NCE) awarding institutions	Less than 90	124
Training of lecturers	Low attention	Federal Government has sponsored 7,000 lecturers of federal and state tertiary institutions for post-graduate studies home and abroad to improve the quality of instruction
Student enrolment in the Colleges of Education	Less than 500,000	Over 750,000

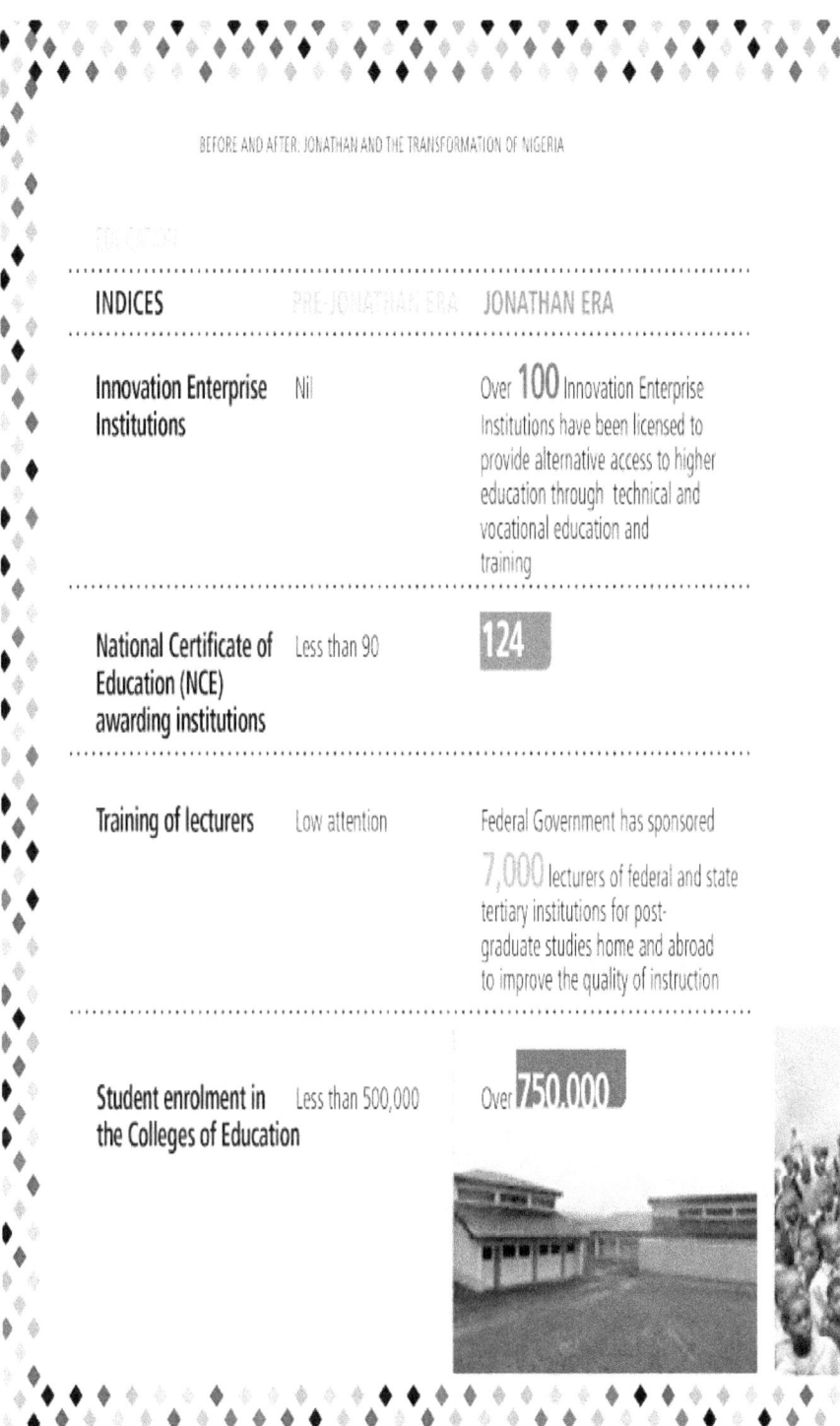

EDUCATION

INDICES	PRE-JONATHAN ERA	JONATHAN ERA
Laboratories in the 51 Federal and State polytechnics	Inadequate and obsolete	**Rehabilitated** with state-of-the-art equipment
Unity Schools	Neglected	In 2013 alone, Federal Government rehabilitated 352 laboratories and constructed 72 new libraries
Micro-teaching laboratories	Nil	Constructed in 58 Federal and state Colleges of Education across the Federation
Budgetary allocations to education	Low	**Doubled**

The Nigeria Mortgage Company will enable up to 200,000 affordable mortgages within the next 5 years.

Over 61,000 housing units are being built in 6 geographical zones to provide affordable and quality homes.

HOUSING

INDICES	PRE-JONATHAN ERA	JONATHAN ERA
Mortgage	Inadequate attention	The Nigerian Mortgage Refinancing Company (NMRC) has been set up to enable up to **200,000** affordable mortgages within five years
Housing construction	Inadequate attention	Over **61,000** housing units have been built in six geopolitical zones to provide affordable and quality houses

Pre-Jonathan Era: 60 million cell phones; 30 million internet users.

Jonathan Era: 120 million cell phones and 60 million internet users.

15 Million in Venture Capital launched for ICT Entrepreneurs.

Local Production of the Tablet similarly to the IPad.

ICT

INDICES	PRE-JONATHAN ERA	JONATHAN ERA
Mobile phones	60 million	**120 million**
Internet users	Less than 30 million	Over **60 million**
e-governance	Low attention	Government currently delivers more than **50** services online, including passport and driving licence application process
Venture Capital for ICT entrepreneurs	Nil	**$15** million fund launched
e-commerce	Fledgling	Nigeria's e-commerce companies, such as Jumia and Konga, are among the fastest growing in the world
IT access at tertiary institutions	Very low	**27** Federal Universities have been connected via 10GBps meshed trunk circuits
National Broadband Policy	Nil	**Launched**

INDICES	PRE-JONATHAN ERA	JONATHAN ERA
Local production of tablets	Nil	Tablets, equivalent to the iPad, developed
Rural phone access	Grossly indequate	Construction of 500km of fibre-optic cable to rural areas, with 3,000km more targeted for deployment in 2014
Computerising schools	On the drawing board	Computing facilities provided to 74 tertiary institutions and 218 public schools across the country

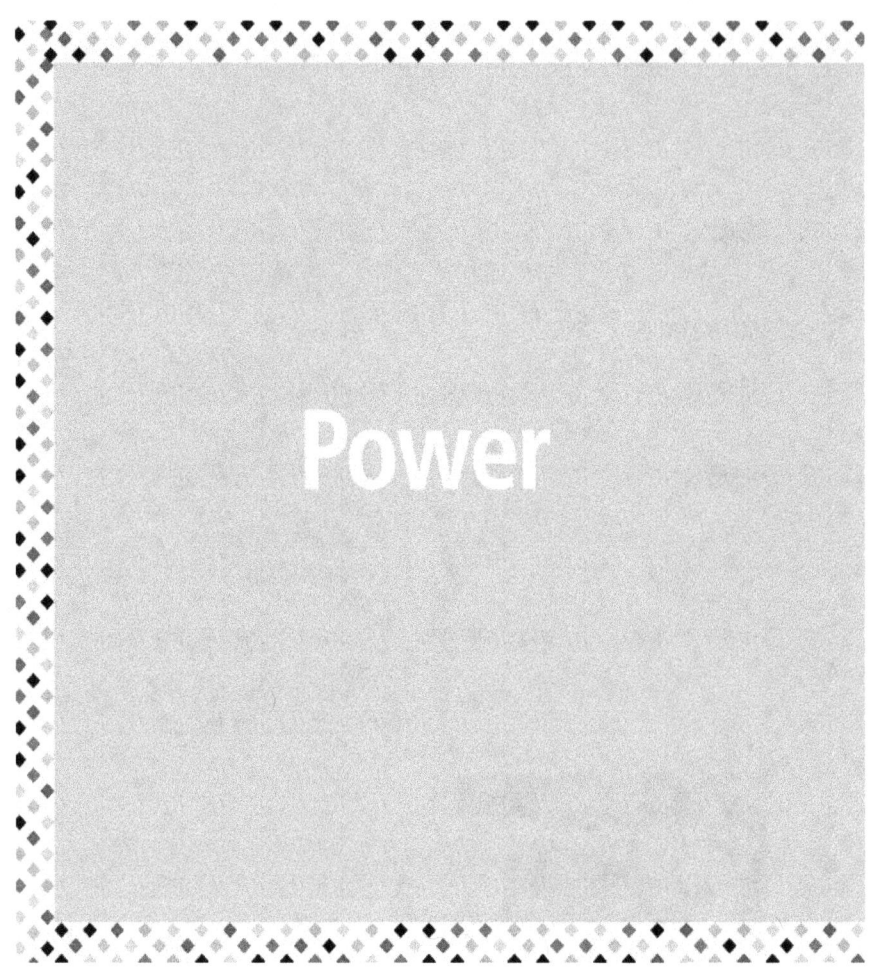

Power

136 Km Gas Pipeline from Oben to the Geregu Power Plant.

31 Km Gas Pipeline from Itoki to Olorunsogo Power Plant.

Solar Power Plants under construction.

Bulk Electricity Trader Established.

LeVonder Pheon Brinkley

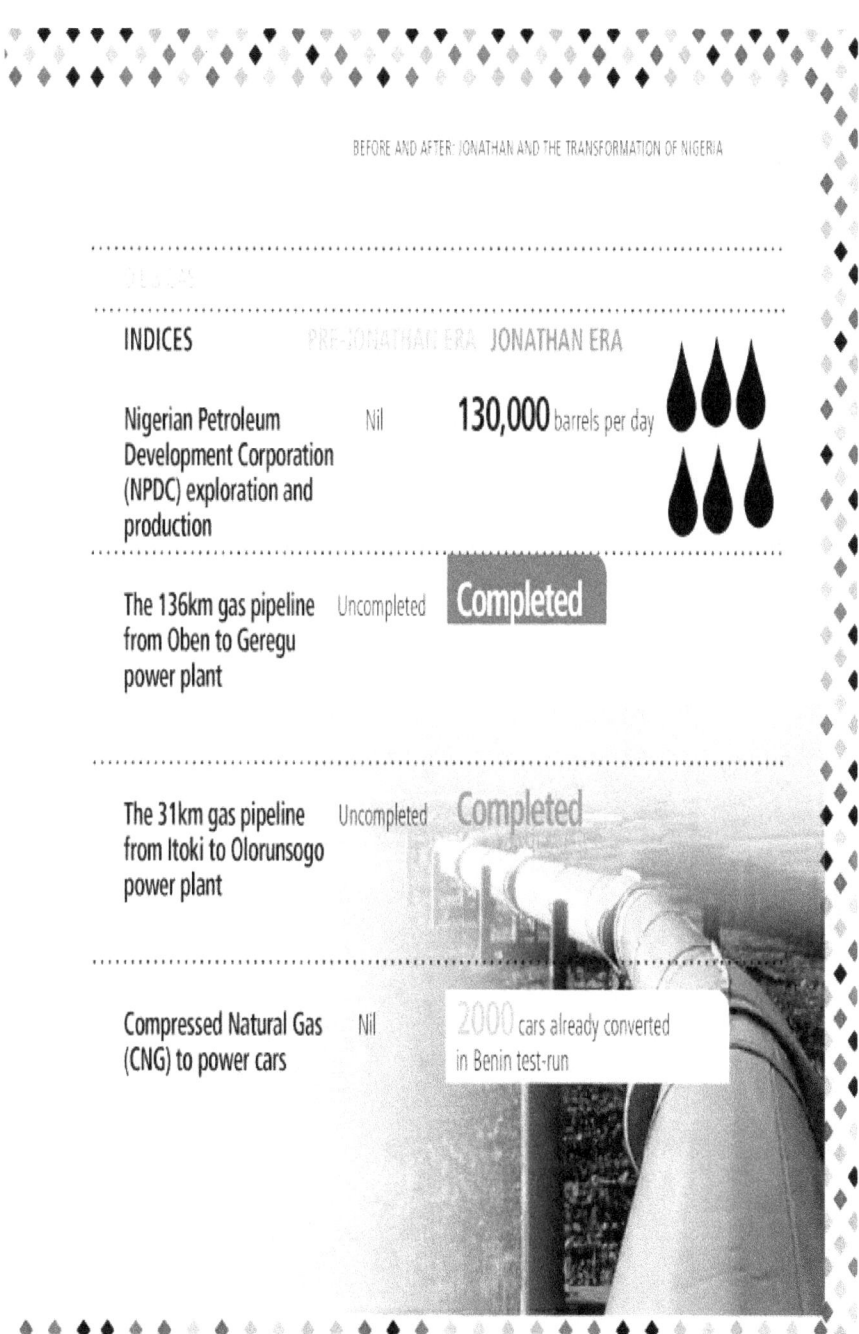

INDICES	PRE-JONATHAN ERA	JONATHAN ERA
Nigerian Petroleum Development Corporation (NPDC) exploration and production	Nil	**130,000** barrels per day
The 136km gas pipeline from Oben to Geregu power plant	Uncompleted	**Completed**
The 31km gas pipeline from Itoki to Olorunsogo power plant	Uncompleted	**Completed**
Compressed Natural Gas (CNG) to power cars	Nil	2000 cars already converted in Benin test-run

POWER

INDICES	PRE-JONATHAN ERA	JONATHAN ERA
Power Sector Road Map	Nil	Launched undergoing implementation
Privatisation of power utility	Conceived	PHCN companies (11 distribution and 6 generation companies) have been successfully privatised and handed over to new owners
Bulk Electricity Trader	Conceived	The Nigeria Bulk Electricity Trader (NBET) has been established to drive private sector investment into the power industry by executing bankable purchase agreements with power developers
Solar power	Nil	Two private sector-led, federal government-backed solar plants of 1000mw each under construction in Yobe and kano states

The Creative Industry

PACT-Project Advancing Creativity and Technology- President Jonathan has set aside a $3 Billion grant for PACT.

BEFORE AND AFTER: JONATHAN AND THE TRANSFORMATION OF NIGERIA

CREATIVE INDUSTRY

INDICES	PRE-JONATHAN ERA	JONATHAN ERA
NEXIM support	Nil	**Available** as an initiative of President Jonathan
Project Advancing Creativity and Technology (PACT) in Nollywood	Nil	**N3 billion** grant set up by President Jonathan

19 years

How long it took the Super Eagles to win another Africa Cup of Nations, having last won it in 1994

ange Africa Cup of Nations
OUTH AFRICA 2013

6,720,000

Number of tree seedlings raised in seven front line states: Adamawa, Bauchi, Jigawa, Yobe, Kebbi, Katsina, Kano, Yobe, Sokoto and Borno States to combat desertification

Super Eagles Won the
World Cup of Nations

BEFORE AND AFTER: JONATHAN AND THE TRANSFORMATION OF NIGERIA

13 years

How long ago Nigeria had not won a medal at the World Athletics Championship until Blessing Okagbare won two at Moscow 2013

7000

Federal Government has sponsored 7,000 lecturers of federal and state tertiary institutions for post-graduate studies home and abroad to improve the quality of instruction since 2011. This is unprecedented.

Blessings Okagbare

Won 2 Cups in Moscow

THE INTERNAL

SECURITY

OF

NIGERIA

A SECURE NATION

I am quite impressed by what I have learned through my research for this publication. President Jonathan has accomplished a lot during his time in office. Some of his efforts are mentioned here in bringing security to the country.

Nigerian National Council of State's Approval of President Jonathan:

The international world has been watching Nigeria for its handling of the kidnapped Chibok Town schoolgirls. The Nigerian National Council of State, comprised of past Presidents, State Governors, and leaders of Parliament, is satisfied that security agents know where the girls are located. The girls will be brought home safely. The military is doing it in a way as not to bring harm or endanger the lives of the girls. The Council is confident that President Jonathan, his National Security Advisors and the Military are on top of the situation.

U.S. officials and Secretary of State John Kerry are working in concert with President Jonathan and are on the ground in Nigeria to help the government find the 219 remaining girls kidnapped by the terrorist group Boko Haram, Secretary of State John Kerry announced, "Our inter-agency team is hitting the ground in Nigeria now, and they are going to be working in concert with President Goodluck Jonathan's government to do everything that we possibly can to return these girls to their families and their communities," Kerry said during an appearance with Syrian Opposition Coalition President Ahmad Jarba.

Commitment to Eliminate All Threats to Internal Security of the Nation.

The Inspector General of Police, **Mohammed Dahiru Abubakar** assumed his position in 2012 during President Jonathan's presidency. Since assumption of office, he has worked tirelessly to reposition the Nigerian Police and to restore public confidence in the Force (FRANK).

The **Nigeria Police Force** (NPF) is the principal law enforcement agency in Nigeria with a staff of around 371,800. According to therichest.com, the NPF ranks as the ninth largest police force in the world and largest in Africa with a ratio of 205 officers per 100,000 citizens (Wikipedia).

The NPF is a very large organization consisting of 36 commands grouped into 12 zones and 6 administrative organs. He has advocated a N50, 000 minimum wage for a constable in the Force, saying such will go a long way to boost morale and promote efficiency. The IG said he had already made proposal to the Federal Government and making a "serious representation" for the actualization of the new salary structure for the police.

He said apart from salary, other welfare packages like housing, training, mortgage policy and efficient cooperative society are being restructured to ensure that every policeman benefits from the scheme. 'We have started with the 500 housing unit in Abuja.'

He warned his men to henceforth stop any form of harassment of journalists and other innocent Nigerians, saying if reports were made, appropriate action will be taken against the erring officer.

He, however, urged them to protect their stations and other public buildings. The IGP further stressed that, "The era of attacking police station or government building is over," said Akubakar.

He said 16,000 policemen out of the 50,000 will go for Intelligence Training, while 10,000 will go for Detective Training. He added that the newly promoted Assistant Inspector Generals of Police underwent a two week management course in Lagos.

He ordered 300 patrol vehicles to be deployed in all the major roads in the country for effective policing and safety of the people on highways. He said all hands must be on deck to ensure the safety of our dear nation (ACP FRANK MBA, http://www.npf.gov.ng/news/reformation-agenda).

Concerned by the incessant terror attacks, herdsmen/farmers clashes in some parts of the country as well as other forms of crimes and criminality – kidnappings, abductions trans-border banditry, proliferation of arms and ammunition – taking place in the country, Inspector-General of Police, Abubakar, convened an emergency meeting with the top echelon of the Police Force, on July 3rd, 2014 at the Force Headquarters Abuja to appraise the overall security situation and the way forward.

While urging the Zonal AIGs and the Command CPs to evolve new intelligence gathering and crime-fighting techniques and methodologies customized to suit their respective local challenges, the IGP charged the senior officers to improve on their surveillance network and high police visibility across the country and to commence early preparations for the 2015 general elections by conducting adequate threat analysis and intensifying capacity building for electoral policing best practices.

The IGP reminded the Police top brass of the immense trust and confidence reposed in them by the public and charged them to bring their professionalism, skills and experience to bear in the discharge of this onerous but statutory mandate of solving crimes, maintaining law and order, protecting lives and property and ridding the country free of terror, amongst others. The IGP reiterated that the country is passing through one of its most trying moments as a nation and therefore demands of its officers, utmost loyalty and commitment to duty. The IGP assured the citizenry of the commitment of the Nigeria Police Force and other security agencies to their well-being, noting that the Forces will continually do their best towards eliminating all threats to internal security of the nation

(Frank, http://www.npf.gov.ng/news/view-news?id=311#.U8a2Y4FdUjA)

Security Forces and Citizens Work in Concert to Control Crime

"...although the war on terrorism is unrelenting, it is certainly not insurmountable and must be won with the cooperation of all," reports the IGP Mohammed Dahiru Abubakar.

Credible intelligence reports at the disposal of the Nigeria Police indicate that terrorists have perfected plot to carry out attacks on the Abuja transport sector. The attacks which are intended to cause panic amongst Abuja residents and visitors alike are planned to be perpetrated through suicide bombings, or through the use of Improvised Explosive Devices (IEDs) concealed in luggage, bags, cans, and other receptacles. The Police High Command therefore, while ordering FCT Commissioner of Police in particular and other CPs in adjoining States to beef-up security at major parks around Abuja and its environs, enjoins the general public, particularly those within and outside the Federal Capital Territory, Abuja to be roundly vigilant and report any suspicious persons, objects, movements or activities to the Security Forces without delay.

Meanwhile, the Police Authorities enjoin citizens not to panic as the Security Forces are working round the clock to neutralize and effectively deal with the threat.

As part of additional efforts at forestalling the attacks and strengthening security around the transport sector, the Police High Command has called on the management of Motor-parks to ensure that travelers and workers' safety comes first. It charges them to constantly conduct regular and routine scanning of their environments while insisting on carrying out a thorough search on passengers and their bags as well as vehicles entering and leaving their parks. It also advises that such searches must have the active participation of the passengers involved and warns that any item or luggage unaccompanied by any passenger must be rejected outright and should not be allowed into the vehicle. Passengers are also enjoined to be on the lookout for any passenger, who might come in with luggage but will attempt to disembark without such luggage.

While operators of motor parks are strongly advised to discourage overnight parking of vehicles at motor parks, particularly by unknown persons, the Police authorities further advise motor park workers to reduce congestion at the parks by disallowing the indiscriminate parking of private cars, tricycles and motorcycles at the precincts of motor parks.

In addition the Police High Command advises that the general public in other places outside the motor parks should also monitor their environments as the terrorists may likely shift attention having known that their plots have been uncovered (Frank, http://www.npf.gov.ng/news/view-news?id=313#.U8a3F4FdUjA).

POLICE UNCOVER PLANS TO ATTACK ABUJA TRANSPORT SERVICE

Following discreet, sustained and painstaking investigation, Police Detectives attached to the Federal Special Anti-Robbery Squad, (FSARS) Force CID Annex, Lagos, smashed a deadly armed robbery gang and arrested key members of the gang in addition to recovering seventeen (17) exotic cars and other exhibits, which they had stolen from different parts of the country. Also recovered from the gang were two (2) locally made single barrel pistols and assorted ammunition.

The Police commenced Investigations into the activities of this notorious gang, which specialized in the robbery of state of the art cars and selling same to unsuspecting members of the public, following a petition by one of their victims who complained that he was robbed of two vehicles and other valuables on the 27th of June, 2013 at his Ile-Ife home.

Consequently, the arrest of one Omoniyi Ajewole, a 28-year-old male from Ilesha and his evidence upon interrogation led to the arrest of other gang members namely: 20 years-old Oluseye Idowu Jacob, who is also from Ilesha in Osun state, Oluwadamilare Rasaki, Ajisafe Olawale, Ogunniyi Sunday, Tolani Babatunde aka Biggy, Abubakar Umar aka Barry, Odeyemi Itunnu aka Gomina and Ayodeji Olumudi.

While commending the Police detectives for their commitment, diligence and professionalism which led to the breakthrough and subsequent recovery of the stolen items, the Inspector-General of Police, IGP MD Abubakar, CFR, NPM, mni, psc enjoined the citizens to continue to support the Police with relevant information, calling on all those who had lost their vehicles in the recent past to come forward with their proof of ownership so as to reclaim them.

Meanwhile, all the suspects connected with the crime will soon be arraigned before a competent court of law for criminal charges preferred against them (Frank, http://www.npf.gov.ng/news/view-news?id=312#.U8a4EoFdUjA).

Following the massive onslaught by Security Forces on the activities of the insurgent group, Boko Haram, at the Balmo Forest Bauchi State, Police detectives attached to Bauchi State Police Command on Saturday, July 12, 2014 about 2pm arrested one Mohammed Zakari, a male of 30 years old and senior member of the Boko Haram terrorists' organization along Darazo-Basrika Road while fleeing from the intensive counter insurgency operations going on around the Balmo Forest. The suspect, who hails from Kaigamari Village, Daptchari in Darazo Local Government Area, Bauchi State is the self-styled "chief butcher" of the insurgent group at the Balmo Forest Camp and is linked with the recent slaughter of seven (7) people, including women and children. Findings as well as disclosures from the suspect will assist the Law enforcement agencies in tracking down some other members of the terror cell.

The suspect whom investigation reveals was tutored in the art of insurgency at Gombe Forest under the leadership of a fleeing insurgent, one Abba Taura and moved to Balmo Forest only three months ago, is discovered to have actively participated in the April attack against Customs officers at Kari Town, along Maiduguri Road, Bauchi State.

Meanwhile, the Police High Command has called on the citizens in the affected areas to be on guard for any suspicious or strange character fleeing from Balmo Forest.

It also calls for the understanding and support of the public for the efforts of the Police and other Security Forces in tackling insurgency, terrorism and other related crimes headlong, noting that although the war on terrorism is unrelenting, it is certainly not insurmountable and must be won with the cooperation of all (Frank, http://www.npf.gov.ng/news/view-news?id=313#.U8a3F4FdUjA).

During President Jonathan's Administration-

The **2014 Recruitment Of Professional Pilots And Engineers Into The Nigeria Police Force**

This is a great addition which will help to ensure internal security as well as *increase employment* among Nigerian citizens.

The following are needed and being hired at the time of this publication:

1. FIXED WING

a. CAPTAINS ONLY

b. CO-PILOTS ONLY

Candidates cannot be more than 28 years of age by the 1st October, 20014.

2. HELICOPTERS

a. CAPTAINS

b. CO-PILOTS ONLY

3. REQUIREMENTS FOR ENGINEERS

Candidates must possess the West African School Certificate 'O' Levels with a minimum of five (5) Credits which must include English Language, Mathematics and Physics and must be graduates of a **Recognized Aviation Training Institution.**

PHYSICAL FITNESS

a. Candidates must not have any physical deformities and will be required to pass a medical examination of physical fitness conducted by a recognized/acceptable government hospital.

b. Be of Good Character.
c. Must be free of pecuniary embarrassment.

The Nigeria Police has posted the following Security Tips for its Citizens on their website-

"You have the primary responsibility to prevent crime against yourself, loved ones and your properties."

Thinking that crime can only happen to someone else and doing nothing to prepare yourself or take precautionary preventive measures, makes you a perfect target for criminals.The ultimate goal of crime prevention is to reduce the risk of being a victim. In order to accomplish this effectively, it is important to remove opportunities for a criminal to take advantage of you or your property.

You are attempting to prevent either victimization or criminalization by presenting an unattractive target to the criminal. This effort at removing opportunities is often referred to as target hardening. Target hardening can be as complex as installing a high tech alarm system or taking a self-defense course to something as simple as locking your door. Making yourself less of a target is simpler than you might think.

These are some of the security tips; the information included in this section provides information to show what you can do to prevent crimes before they happen:

Home Safety Tips

1. Make sure there are good locks on exterior doors and windows.

2. Lock up when you go out, are asleep, or alone, even if it is only for a few minutes. It takes a thief ten seconds or less to enter an open room and steal your property.

3. Trim flowers that hide doorways or windows.

4. Set timers on lights and radios to make your home appear lived-in when you are away.

5. Have a neighbor regularly check on your home when you are away and report any suspicious activities (Good turn deserves another)

6. Mark your valuables with a number or identification unique to you, with an engraving pen and keep a list of them in a safe place.

7. Get to know your neighbors and their daily routines.

8. Keep a list of emergency numbers, especially of the police station close to you.

9. Make sure your home is fenced, and if you can afford it, you can have a smart security guard.

10. Trim bushes to less than 3 feet to eliminate possible hiding places, especially near windows and sidewalks

11. Trim tree canopies to at least 8 feet to allow visibility into your property. Replace solid walls in front yards with open fencing to eliminate hiding places and make climbing more difficult.

12. Install a wide-angle peephole in your front door so you can look out to an oncoming visitor without being seen yourself.

13. Do not give out information about your neighbors.

14. Do not make it easy on burglars.

15. Keep valuables away from windows

ATM SECURITY TIPS

Be alert and conscious of your surroundings when using the ATM.

Don't use an ATM machine located in a dark or obscure location

Never give your card or PIN (Personal Identification Number) to anyone, for any reason.

Be very conscious of persons hanging around the ATM machine don't write your PIN on the card or anything that is kept with the card.

Do not insert your card until asked to do so by the display screen

Never use an ATM with a blank screen and, if the ATM is obscured from view or poorly lit, leave immediately and find another ATM.

Stand close to the ATM and use your body and hand as shield to make sure nobody sees you keying in your pin

Never accept help from strangers when using an ATM. You should be wary of strangers asking for help. The elderly or physically challenged persons should take along with them trusted persons to assist them.

Criminals work in teams- one to distract you while the other steals your card or money.

If your card is retained (swallowed) by the ATM it is advisable to contact your bank immediately

It is advisable to set a daily ATM withdrawal limit on your account.

Sign up for SMS alert, so that you are alerted whenever any withdrawal is made in your account

Vehicle Security Tips

Most car crime is preventable. Police are making a concerted effort to tackle car crime and target offenders, but motorists need to help themselves avoid becoming victims by removing the opportunity for crime in the first place.

1. Don't leave anything on display - it's a prime invitation to passersby. Even an old coat or plastic bag can tempt a thief. If items have to be left in the car, put them out of sight at the start of your journey

2. Get a music system that's removable or has a front that can be taken off and remove iPods and MP3 players

3. Driving documents and personal correspondence could help a thief to sell your vehicle or provide a cover story if stopped by the police - do not keep these in your vehicle

4. Some car thieves break into houses to steal car keys. Always keep the keys in a safe place. Don't leave them in the hallway or kitchen, as these are the obvious places.

Police can be reached on the following hot lines:

- **FCT Police Control, Rm. – 07057337653**
- **Force Intelligence Bureau Operations Room - 08139379245**

PEACE

INITIATIVES

IN NIGERIA

Peace

A tremendous amount of work is being done in the country of Nigeria in the name of Peace. Peace is the by-product of a secure country, both internally and internationally. Providing public safety and security is the most fundamental responsibility of a government, but the government cannot do it without the aid of the people. President Jonathan's administration has and continues to work diligently to provide security and safety. He has requested of the people to take responsibility and to be accountable as well.

One such organization that is made up of citizens is the Universal Peace Federation. The Universal Peace Federation of Nigeria's Secretary General Raphael Oko is working tirelessly to bring Peace to his country. In preparing for the observance of the UN International Day of Peace, Sept. 21, 2014, UPF-Nigeria invites nominations of Nigerians who love peace and set an example as global citizens transcending religion and ethnic nationality. Each approved nominee will receive a letter of recognition from UPF-Nigeria and a copy of the UPF founder's autobiography, *As a Peace-Loving Global Citizen.* Nominations should be sent to nigeria@upf.org.

The majority of Nigerians are peace-loving and peaceful. Many aspire to live as global citizens. A few have become terrorists and an insignificant number are still promoting the idea of indigenes and non-indigenes. In an era of democratic governance where government is by majority decision for the people and by the people, it is unfair to use the activities of few terrorists and ethnic champions to describe Nigeria negatively. This campaign seeks to demonstrate that Nigerians are peace-loving global citizens.

The Universal Peace Federation (UPF) is a global network of individuals and organizations dedicated to building a world of peace centered on universal spiritual and moral values. The author of this publication participated in the first anniversary of the passing of the founder of UPF and the commemoration of the International Inter-religious Conference in Seoul South Korea along with Nigerian and other ambassadors from 80 countries and 8 major religions.

As part of activities related to the commemoration of the second anniversary of the peaceful passing of the UPF Founder, Dr. Sun Myung Moon (1920 – 2012) and in commemoration of the UN International Day of Peace on September 21, 2014, the office of the secretary general of UPF-Nigeria has commenced a "Peace-Loving Global Citizen Campaign" in Abuja with a strong appeal to Nigerians to become peace-loving global citizens as a way to overcome the present violence and security challenges in the country.

The campaign involves a one–to–one distribution of the the founder's autobiography, *As a Peace-Loving Global Citizen,* to area council chairmen, business leaders, heads of educational institutions, civil and political leaders, and other persons in strategic positions of leadership. This is an opportunity to connect people with information, each other and resources for peace-building. The founder's autobiography has been a source of inspiration to many Ambassadors for Peace in Nigeria. It is hoped that by distributing the book to leaders and holding small-group reading sessions at the Peace Embassy, the heart of the nation can be moved to make a strong commitment to peace.

Being aware that Nigeria is currently facing severe challenges in inter-ethnic relations, where state of origin has become more important than the nation, where people prefer to be indigenes of tribes instead of citizens of the nation, this campaign seeks to raise up a unique group advocating for a new way of life. The campaign enjoins each person to become peaceful and also to strive to become a global citizen, regarding others as brothers and sisters, transcending all differences.

The campaign in Abuja began with the presentation of an Ambassador for Peace certificate and the founder's autobiography to Mr. Mohammed Abdul Najeeb, speaker, journalist and board member of Speakers Council of India, based in Abuja. As the campaign intensifies, it is hoped that people's perspective will advance from being warring indigenes of tribes to become peace-loving global citizens, recognizing that the age of independent nationality is evolving into an age of global interdependent citizenship.

Peace Clubs in all Colleges- The executive secretary of the National Commission for Colleges in Education has approved the request for partnership by UPF Nigeria to establish Peace Clubs in all the colleges of education in Nigeria. The approval was contained in a letter to the secretary general of UPF-Nigeria dated June 11, 2014 in response to the UPF-Nigeria letter to the Commission dated 20 January 2014. The letter signed by ag director, Academic Programs Department of the Commission, Muhammad Sani Aliyu, for the executive secretary states that "I am directed to inform you that the Executive Secretary has approved that we (NCCE) partner with the Universal Peace Federation" for the purposes of establishing peace clubs in the colleges.

By this approval, we shall be working together with the commission to ensure that Peace Clubs are established in all the colleges of education in Nigeria. The colleges of education are the formal educational institutions responsible for the training of teachers for primary and junior secondary schools in Nigeria. The commission is looking forward to working together to create Peace Clubs in the over 80 colleges of education as well as introduction of peace education in the colleges in the days ahead. The list of colleges of education in Nigeria is available online.

Abuja, Nigeria - **The UN World Day for Cultural Diversity for Dialogue and Development was commemorated in Abuja on May 23, 2014,** with a special leadership convocation at the Yaradua International Conference Center. Participants included Ambassadors of Argentina, Sudan, Tanzania and Niger Republic to Nigeria with several Ambassadors for Peace, women leaders, government representatives from the Federal Road Safety Commission, National Universities Commission, Federal Ministry of Women Affairs and Social Development, and the State Security Service among others.

(In December 2002, the UN General Assembly declared May 21 to be the World Day for Cultural Diversity for Dialogue and Development in order to provide "an opportunity to deepen our understanding of the values of cultural diversity and to learn to live together better.)

The message of the president of the UN General Assembly was read by Robert Okere, a Nigeria Ambassador for Peace in Ireland: "On this World Day for Cultural Diversity for Dialogue and Development, I encourage all of us to recognize the importance of cultural diversity, both as a reflection of the richness of humankind, and as essential to the flourishing of countries and communities across the world. As we approach 2015, the international community is seeking to identify ways to promote inclusive socio-economic development across the world. Development needs to be truly sustainable and should be adapted to local contexts; it should rely on the cultural resources of countries and peoples, while respecting cultural rights."

Amb. (Dr.) Aisha Audu-Emeje, wife of the former governor of Kogi State, read the message of UNESCO Director General Irina Bokova: "Our cultural diversity is a stimulator of creativity. Investing in this creativity can transform societies. It is our responsibility to develop education and intercultural skills in young people to sustain the diversity of our world and to learn to live together in the diversity of our languages, cultures and religions, to bring about change."

A special presentation on the Path to National Peace and Unification: UPF Vision 2020 was presented by Dr Raphael Ogar Oko, secretary general of UPF-Nigeria.

Goodwill messages were delivered by ambassadors to Nigeria from Argentina, Niger, Sudan and Tanzania as well as the executive secretary of the National Universities Commission, chief of staff of the Nigerian Army Headquarters, the minister of Women's Affairs and

Social Development, and the Corps Marshall/CEO of the Federal Road Safety Corps. Ambassador for Peace certificates were presented to the four ambassadors in attendance and 12 other distinguished participants. The event was reported on national radio and TV.

Uyo, Akwa Ibom State, Nigeria - Ambassadors for Peace commemorated the UN International Day of Families with a conference on "Families Matter on Achieving the Development Goals" on May 15, 2014. Participants in the conference included Ambassadors for Peace, religious and local traditional leaders, public civil servants, youth leaders and government representatives. Over 500 persons attended the one-day conference that was declared open by Executive Governor of Akwa Ibom State Godswill Akpabio, who was represented by the State Commissioner for Information.

The conference at the Akwa Ibom State Government Civil Service Auditorium, Idongesit Nkanga Secretariat featured discussions on the family as the school of human development and peace as well as promoting national unity through strong marriages and families. The conference chairman, Hon. Joe Offong, spoke on the significance of the family and called on all Ambassadors for Peace to make a sincere commitment to building strong and peaceful families as a tool for the realization of world peace. His opening remarks were followed by a special presentation of "We Are One Human Family under God" by an Akwa Ibom state based interdenominational choir group.

The UN Secretary-General's message was read by Una B. Smart from the UPF-Nigeria Happy Health Wellness

Center in Abuja. According to Secretary-General Ban Ki-moon, "As we commemorate this year's International Day of Families, we recognize the meaningful contributions that families make to advancing the mission of the United Nations" Mr. Ban called for mobilizing the world's families as countries strive to usher in a more sustainable future, achieve the Millennium Development Goals, shape a new development agenda and combat climate change.

"By providing economic and emotional sustenance to their members, families can raise productive, caring citizens committed to the common good. Strong, well-functioning families, whatever form they may take, can help reduce poverty, improve the wellbeing of mothers, promote gender equality and uphold human rights. Let us strive to strengthen these small but critical units found in every society so that we may advance as one human family toward greater progress"

The UPF-Nigeria Zonal Coordinator for Cross River, Akwa Ibom and Abia States, William S. Williams read the UPF recommendation on the need to strengthen families, which are stated below:

First, Universal Peace Federation acknowledges that the family is a microcosm of the global community. If the world is to finally come to an era of sustainable peace and harmony among civilizations, that peace must be founded on this basic, most intimate social unit of humankind. In other words, the family is the central building block of society, as well as being an instrument for peace and reconciliation.

Second, the family is universal. Regardless of race, ethnicity, nationality, and religious affiliations, we are all members of families. Most importantly, the family is the school of love and ethics. Through experiences in our families, we learn to embrace and value all relationships in our wider human family; with friends, neighbors, co-workers, colleagues and strangers.

Third, marriage, parenting, and the family are the basis of human development and the core institutions for education in character, ethics, social relationships, and citizenship. Strong, healthy, loving parents and families help protect society from the moral decline of its youth, increase in crime, drug abuse and corruption, as well as the spread of diseases such as HIV/AIDS. In addition, they can help break down the age-old resentments that have fuelled religious, tribal, and civil conflict.

Fourth, throughout history, the family has experienced economic and social unrest, and its adaptability is now being threatened by a wide range of social, economic, cultural, and political developments. UPF chapters around the world are focusing on projects to overcome poverty and social exclusion within families and have been mindful to include underprivileged or marginalized groups in their programs. UPF includes wide representation of the various faith groups in its policies and projects.

Fifth, lasting peace is secured not merely through laws, backed by the power of government enforcement, but by a rising awareness of our universal solidarity as one human family, brothers and sisters who share a common spiritual and moral heritage. We are one family under God.

Governor Akpabio paid special tribute to the UPF founders for their commitment toward bringing all people and nations together to live in peace on earth and even in heaven. "We will work with the UPF and all people of the world to build one global family under God," he said. The governor also called on all Nigerians to continue to pray for the release of the abducted girls of the Chibok School in northeast Nigeria.

The keynote lecture was delivered by Dr. Raphael Ogar Oko, Secretary General of UPF-Nigeria, on "The Family and the Millennium Development Goals," in which he emphasized the significance of the family as the universal school of peace and the institution for sustainable development and love. "All the goals of the MDGs can be achieved if we make them our Family Development Goals. Eradication of extreme poverty and hunger begins from the family. The family is the best institution for achieving basic education while the promotion of gender equality and empowerment of women must begin from our families. Our families should take up the responsibility of reducing child mortality and the improvement of maternal health. We can only win the war against HIV/AIDS when we have strong families who practice chastity before marriage and fidelity in marriage. If we realize that our society is our family, we will not waste the resources in our environment. Partnership for development begins from partnership between men and women, parents and children, among siblings, etc. In fact, the family is the school where we learn and practice the principles that can help achieve the MDGs."

This presentation was followed by a general discussion on the place of the family in achieving the MDGs as well as national unification of Nigeria. Ambassadors for Peace renewed their commitment to building stable families and a draft of the outline of activities to achieve the National Unification Initiative was presented and endorsed by the participants at the conference. At the closing session, special awards were presented to the oldest Ambassadors for Peace for their work in strengthening families in their communities. Hon. Lukpata, a member of the Cross River State House of Assembly, received the UPF Nigeria medal as the most supportive Ambassador for Peace of the April 2014 membership drive.

At the closing session, participants commended the United Nations for the International Day of Families' initiative and also commended the UPF founders for their lifelong work for world peace through loving families. They called on the government to create the Ministry of Family Affairs and establish a National Institute for Marriage as well as appealed for the introduction and marriage and family education in all tertiary educational institutions in Nigeria.

Twenty-seven new Ambassadors for Peace were inducted and presented certificates as part of the closing session. In recognition of the outstanding accomplishment of Governor Godswill Akpabio, the Ambassadors for Peace moved that the UPF Leadership and Good Governance award be presented to him in a later date and a special commendation letter as a "Family-Friendly Governor" be sent to him by UPF-Nigeria.

The event in Uyo was organized in partnership with the Akwa Ibom State chapter of the Family Federation for World Peace and Unification and received media coverage by both private and government owned radio and TV stations and the local newspapers.

Abuja, Nigeria - The Nigeria chapter of the Universal Peace Federation has launched a special initiative to connect Nigerians around the world to ongoing efforts to build a peaceful Nigeria nation by the year 2020. In response to the increasing violence and insecurity in Nigeria, UPF-Nigeria launched the special initiative to connect Nigerians in diaspora to peace initiatives in Nigeria. The launch took place in Abuja on April 30, 2014 in a special dinner for peace held at the Peace Embassy.

The launch featured the commissioning of Babatunde Lawal Abbas, a Nigerian based in Japan, as a Nigerian Ambassador for Peace in Japan with the mandate to use his new calling to reach out to the Nigerian community in Japan and identify people who can be commissioned as Ambassadors for Peace to work to support the UPF in Japan as well as peace initiatives in Nigeria.

The event was graced by four Japanese volunteers who have been working with the Nigeria chapter of the Family Federation for World Peace and Unification and the Universal Peace Federation in Abuja. The program featured a special musical entertainment by Mrs. Takako Alao, a Japanese married to a Nigerian, with congratulatory messages by Rev George Ogurie, Rotarian Olaleye Alao, and Dr. George C. Ikpot. They commended the dedication of Babatunde Lawal Abbas and his keen interest to serve his country.

At the award presentation ceremony, Dr. Raphael Ogar Oko, Secretary General of UPF-Nigeria, described the Nigerian Ambassadors for Peace in Diaspora initiative and called on Nigerians in Diaspora to join in addressing the challenges that Nigeria is facing. "We are hopeful that more Nigerians in diaspora will embrace this initiative both to serve as Ambassadors for Peace in their country of residence and to support efforts in their country of birth. This initiative seeks to connect Nigerians in diaspora to peace building efforts in Nigeria. We have a huge community of Nigerians in every country in the world. We need innovative strategies to engage them positively in contributing to the task of rebuilding our nation."

The Nigerian Ambassadors for Peace in Diaspora initiative began with the commissioning of four Nigerians in diaspora during the special commemorative conference to mark Nigeria's 100th anniversary of national amalgamation. During the event, two Nigerians in Ireland and a Nigerian in the USA with another in the UK were commissioned as Ambassadors for Peace.

Robert Okere and Vicky Robert Okere are very enterprising Nigerians based in Ireland, while Sunday Omagu Ogar, based in the USA and Paulina Morphy Fogg, based in Manchester- UK were also inducted. With the formal launch of the initiative at the Peace Embassy in Abuja, a movement has begun to reach out to Nigerians all over the world and mobilize them to support peace building efforts in Nigeria. Other Nigerians in diaspora can join this growing initiative by contacting UPF Nigeria via _ nigeria@upf.org.

Benue State, Nigeria - In response to its appeal for support in providing emergency food and medical aid to victims of violence, UPF-Nigeria has received donations from Ambassadors for Peace and on April 28, 2014, presented thousands of yams to help feed internally displaced persons in Makurdi, Benue state.

Abuja, Nigeria - A personal appeal by the secretary general of UPF-Nigeria to help enable UPF and its network of Ambassadors for Peace to provide food and medical care to bombing victims and to set up community peace education centers.

Abuja, Nigeria - A commemoration of the 100th anniversary of the amalgamation of Nigeria at the National Merit Award House in Abuja on April 14, 2014, was attended by Ambassadors for Peace and other distinguished Nigerians.

Nairobi, Kenya - Twenty-five Nigerian Ambassadors for Peace traveled to Kenya to join UPF leaders from Benin, Uganda, Somalia, Eritria and Kenya for a Special Leadership Conference March 27–29, 2014 following up on the leadership conference in Korea the previous month.

Abuja, Nigeria - UPF-Nigeria observed the 2014 UN International Day for the Elimination of Racial Discrimination with a seminar at the Peace Embassy in Abuja on March 21, 2014.

Uyo, Akwa Ibom State, Nigeria - Ambassadors for Peace launched a campaign in Akwa Ibom State Feb. 28, 2014, proclaiming 2014 as a year for national unity and emphasizing the significance of marriage and family in building a peaceful nation and world.

Abuja, Nigeria - As Nigeria commemorates 100 years (1914 - 2014) of unity in diversity, UPF-Nigeria will be celebrating Nigeria @ 100 with the appointment of 100 outstanding Nigerians and their spouses as Ambassadors for Peace on April 14, 2014 at the Main Auditorium of the National Merit Award House in Maitama, Abuja. The 100 Ambassadors for Peace shall be commissioned and mobilized as a UPF-Nigeria national unity committee.

Abuja, Nigeria - UPF-Nigeria convened a Special Interreligious Assembly on Feb. 5 to mark World Interfaith Harmony Week 2014 at the Peace Embassy in Abuja and deliberated on innovative approaches to promoting interreligious harmony for the national unity in Nigeria. The event brought together Islamic and Christian religious educators, leaders and organizations to reflect on the challenges of interreligious relations that Nigeria has been facing and what needs to be done to create the much-needed culture, structure and infrastructure for interreligious cooperation and harmony.

Abuja, Nigeria - As Nigeria prepares to commemorate the 100th anniversary of the colonial amalgamation of the nation in 1914, UPF-Nigeria launched a national campaign on Dec. 12, 2013 urging all Nigerians to work toward the unity of the nation ridden by religious and ethnic barriers.

Las Vegas, USA - Delegations from Mali, Nigeria and Guinea Bissau visited Las Vegas in 2013 to discuss concepts related to peace and conflict resolution, study UPF's principles of peace and experience the area's wonders of nature and human creation.

Abuja, Nigeria - An Ambassadors for Peace Seminar on National Dialogue was convened on Oct. 22, 2013, with the theme "Exposition of an Innovative Framework for Sustainable National Dialogue."

Las Vegas, USA - A seminar for Nigerian Ambassadors for Peace on "Building World Peace through the Family Peace Blessing" took place in Las Vegas, USA, Oct.- 27 through Nov. 3. It offered Ambassadors for Peace who represent diverse sections of society the insights, resources and status needed to address marriage and family issues.

Abuja, Nigeria - A National Peacebuilding Convocation on September 21 at the National Merit Award House in Abuja attended by more than 600 people featured a keynote speech on "The Role of Education in Building a Culture of Peace and Fostering Global Citizenship" by Mr. Charles Chibo, an educator, scholar, and international human resources management trainer.

Junaid Abdul Quadri quoted:

"Education has, over the decades, established its importance in the development of any nation. The trend of leadership and scope of management would bring out efficiencies if the leaders are well equipped with informa tion. Those who cease to learn have been considered as those who cease to develop.

This is the reason it is important to inform any youth , who are generally regarded as the future ambassador of any community that striving for education today is equipping yourself to be a leader   tomorrow. Since education and knowledge of technical know-how are instruments of empowering them for the leadership skills and proficiencies.

There is great need for moral and ethical education generally in today's society, particularly in our nation, Nigeria. Why this is so can be understood by reflecting briefly on current social conditions and then more specifically the manner in which education has contributed to them. While not a panacea, education has an important responsibility in fostering the health of any society (spiritual health, mental health, material health and economic health).

The Universal Peace Federation is strong in the country of Nigeria. I urge citizens who are active in bringing about Peace in your community to please contact:

Raphael Oko,
Secretary General, Universal Peace Federation- Nigeria

25 Bujumbura Street
Off Libreville Cresent, by Mr. Biggs Restaurant
Abuja, Wuse II, Nigeria
nigeria@upf.org
+234 805 996 4018

CONCLUSION

Akintokunbo Adejumo, founder and global coordinator of CHAMPIONS FOR NIGERIA, remarked in a speech, "when we say security, are we talking about food insecurity, financial insecurity, personal security, and national security. To end this presentation, allow me to quote former Head of State, Abdulsalaam Abubakar from his guest lecture at NIPSS, Kuru, on November 26, 2004," and he concluded:

> Democracy is a sought-after value. It is not a perfect system of governance, even theoretically. But as Aristotle argued, it is the least evil of all possible governments. The strength of democracy is drawn from the fact that it is supposed to be the product of the will of the majority of the people. Government is held in trust for the people. The citizens feel a sense of ownership of the state when they can identify with it as vital stakeholders whose will gave existence and legitimacy to the state and the government. As shareholders of the common-wealth, the citizens will not only avoid such behaviors that hurt and sabotage the system, but join forces to resist any such attack on the collective interest. That in-fact is the real basis for the development of grand tactic, the mobilization of the entire national asset for the protection of the nation, which I believe can work best in a democracy".

I am moved by the words of Akintokunbo Adejumo and Abdulsalaam Abubakar. I am also moved by the message of the president of the UN General Assembly read on the World Day for Cultural Diversity for Dialogue and Development. The message was read by Robert Okere, a Nigerian Ambassador for Peace in Ireland:

> On this World Day for Cultural Diversity for Dialogue and Development, I encourage all of us to recognize the importance of cultural diversity, both as a reflection of the richness of humankind, and as essential to the flourishing of countries and communities across the world. As we approach 2015, the international community is seeking to identify ways to promote inclusive socio-economic development across the world. Development needs to be truly sustainable and should be adapted to local contexts; it should rely on the cultural resources of countries and peoples, while respecting cultural rights.

H.E. President Goodluck Jonathan's Transformation Agenda resonates with each of these Nigerian citizens. The journey is just beginning. He has done much in transforming the country to one that is secure, peaceful and stabilized in all areas of development. I attempted to highlight some, but they are too many to cover. It is our responsibility to develop education and intercultural skills in young people to sustain the diversity of our languages, cultures and religions to bring about transformation.

Our cultural diversity is a stimulator of creativity. Investing in this creativity can transform societies. I see a Nigeria where all citizens work, recreate, worship and dwell together without regard for gender, age, religious, or tribal differences. They live in PEACE, in a STABILIZED AND DEVELOPED Nation free of fear, but SECURE and filled with compassion for each other. This is the nation that President Jonathan envisioned years ago, and his TRANSFORMATION AGENDA has begun to bring into fruition. Let's lend our support to ensure the Vision of this Transformational Leader.

"Working within the global village is tough.
We sometimes do not even know what time it is 'over there'
where our counterparts live.
Sometimes it seems that life is getting harder as the vehicle
of Transformation is taking us to some destination.
Just remember, hills that are very high become smaller and
smaller when we are climbing them.
We will keep climbing until the hill disappears.
We will reach our destination-
'Global Peace'."

Dr. Frederick Nwosu

President, Emmanuel University

Epilogue

I love the people of my African ancestry. I feel a strong kinship with you. Seth Kaplan, CEO of Corporate Warrior Consulting and I work with Kate Ijoli of Standard Consulting, a firm based in Nigeria. Kate contracted Corporate Warrior Consulting to work with Administrators from the Federal Capital Territory Administration. We shared American based empowerment programs that could empower the women and children in Nigeria. They were very impressed by the Housing for Humanity for Women, and the Youth Build Education program for High School students. It is my desire that you coordinate with Kate Ijoli of Standard Consulting and the administrators to implement some of these programs in Nigeria for Women and Youth Empowerment.

As an Ambassador for Peace, I have collaborated with Ambassadors from Nigeria and other African nations. It is my desire that you coordinate with Raphael Oko, Secretary General of the Universal Peace Federation-Nigeria and get the Nigerian citizens involved with this great work for national and world peace.

Healthcare is a challenge everywhere. I am more than impressed with your gains in saving lives. In addition to saving lives, Healthcare is a way to create jobs and to develop a middle class population to stabilize an economy. All educational levels are needed to carry out healthcare initiatives. I am a board member of a healthcare conglomerate who desires to have a gigantic presence in Nigeria. We have revolutionary healthcare products such as a 360 degree mammogram scanner which weighs less than 8 pounds and can be carried into rural villages for early detection and prevention of breast cancer, plasma activate water for humans, animals, plants and sterilization, and other healthcare technology. See more by going to the website at www.raghala.com and contacting me if you have an interest.

My email address is levonderb@gmail.com.

Corporate Warrior Consulting is available to assist you in any country. It has been a pleasure writing this work to enlighten you of your Transformational Leader-The H.E. President Goodluck Ebele Jonathan.

Respectfully,
Dr. LeVonder Pheon Brinkley, Best –Selling Author

The Transformational Leader
Burn with Passion to Journey on Purpose
The "D" Word- DISCIPLINE
The Gifts- Forgiveness, Unconditional Love, and
Unconditional Acceptance
Daily Action and Gratitude Journals I, II, III, and IV

and Co-author of –
Wake Up...Live the Life You Love with Drs. Wayne Dyer and Deepak Chopra (Best-Selling Series)

levonderb@gmail.com
919-730-8390

www.ingramcontent.com/pod-product-compliance
Lightning Source LLC
Chambersburg PA
CBHW081223280526
45787CB00006B/2502